CW00516710

LAST OF THE DUTY FREE

LAST OF THE DUTY FREE

by Eric Chappell

JOSEF WEINBERGER PLAYS

LONDON

LAST OF THE DUTY FREE
First published in 2015
by Josef Weinberger Ltd
12-14 Mortimer Street, London W1T 3JJ
www.josef-weinberger.com / plays@jwmail.co.uk

ISBN: 978 0 85676 347 2

Printed by Berforts Information Press Ltd, Stevenage

LAST OF THE DUTY FREE was first performed at the Theatre Royal, Windsor on 15th April, 2014 prior to a national UK tour, produced by Bill Kenwright Ltd. The cast was as follows:

DAVID	Keith Barron
LINDA	Carol Royle
CARLOS	Graham Elwell
CLARE	Maxine Gregory
JEREMY	James Barron
AMY	Gwen Taylor
ROBERT	Neil Stacey

Directed by Roger Redfarn

Set and costumes designed by Julie Godfrey

Lighting designed by Douglas Kuhrt

CAST

in order of appearance:

DAVID	Fifties
LINDA	Late forties
CARLOS	A waiter, fifties
CLARE	Newly-wed, thirties
JEREMY	Newly-wed, thirties
AMY	Fifties
ROBERT	Fifties

Photo by Julie Godfrey

ACT ONE

Scene One

The San Remo Hotel. Marbella. Evening.

A split set.

Upstage right is a raised balcony screened from the rest of the apartment by French doors and curtains. The balcony is fronted by iron railings that extend off stage. It is furnished with table and chairs. Below the balcony is a path which leads from stage right to a sun terrace stage left.

The terrace extends upstage and is fronted by a low wall. There is an exit upstage and a further exit midstage which leads down to the rest of the hotel. The terrace is furnished with tables and chairs and three sun loungers have been erected facing upstage as if to catch the most of the sun. A large impenetrable bush decorates the terrace.

Sounds of revelry off.

DAVID PEARCE *is alone on the terrace. He is studying the buttons on his jacket and attempting to get them to meet. Finds them an inch short. He shrugs and gives up. He leaves the jacket open. He then discovers with alarm that his shirt buttons aren't meeting too well either. He expands his stomach and studies the effect. He breaks off when he hears an approach.*

DAVID   (*turns*) Come and look at the view, Harry. That's Africa out there – so close you can almost hear the coconuts dropping . . .

               (LINDA *appears from behind the bush. She is elegantly coifered and expensively dressed.*)

LINDA   Why Harry?

DAVID   How do you think I got away?

LINDA   I did wonder.

DAVID   I'm here with a sick friend. Harry Moffat
           – he needed a change of scene and his wife
           won't travel.

LINDA   And Amy believed that?

DAVID   I can be very persuasive . . .

LINDA   I know – you persuaded me . . .

           (*They embrace. A light flashes.*)

DAVID   What was that? Someone's taking pictures!

LINDA   Probably publicity shots – for the hotel . . .

DAVID   Well, as long as we don't finish up in the
           brochure. That could take some explaining.

LINDA   They won't put us in the brochure, David
           – not without asking. (*Pause.*) Didn't Amy
           want to come?

DAVID   Of course. But she works for Broadbents –
           the butchers – and he's short-staffed. I chose
           my moment carefully.

LINDA   Suppose she checks up?

DAVID   She can't – she doesn't know where Harry
           lives – I don't know where he lives. I haven't
           seen him in years.

LINDA   You've thought of everything. You're very
           smooth aren't you, David.

DAVID   As silk.

               (*They embrace again.* DAVID *feels that she is
               tense. Studies her.*)

               Are you nervous?

LINDA   We've done this before, David and Amy
               found out. She pushed a cream cake in my
               face.

DAVID   That was over twenty years ago.

LINDA   It may have been but I can still taste it.
               What did you tell the people on the plane? A
               man travelling alone?

DAVID   I said I'd recently been bereaved . . .

LINDA   (*smiles*) That's rather moving, isn't it?

DAVID   Yes. One or two people shed a tear. What
               did you tell the people in the bar? I saw you
               talking to them.

LINDA   I said my husband was in Rome on business
               and that I was meeting him at the end of the
               week but that I thought I'd snatch a few days
               in Spain en route.

DAVID   That could just be true.

LINDA   It is true.

DAVID   Oh. Then we haven't got long.

LINDA   Long enough . . .

               (*Another embrace.*)

DAVID	Does he know you've come here?
LINDA	Oh, yes.
DAVID	But he doesn't suspect?
LINDA	Good heavens, no. Why do you ask?
DAVID	It's just that the last time we met . . . the very last time . . .
LINDA	Yes?
DAVID	He said if he ever caught us together again he'd kill me.
LINDA	Did he really?
DAVID	I don't suppose he meant it.
LINDA	No, he'd mean it.
DAVID	At the time but it was all those years ago. I don't think he'd mean it now. It was in the heat of the moment.
LINDA	Not with Robert. He can bear a grudge.
DAVID	He can? I didn't know that.
LINDA	Robert believes that revenge is a dish best eaten cold.
DAVID	I know but things said in temper . . .
LINDA	That doesn't make any difference to Robert. He is, I'm afraid, a man of his word. If he said he'd kill you if he found us together that's exactly what he'd do. And his moods become more unpredictable every year.

DAVID	They do?
LINDA	Yes. I always know when they're coming on. Those large hands of his start opening and closing like this . . .

(She demonstrates, opening and closing her hands. DAVID watches uncomfortably.)

DAVID	But Robert's not a fool – I've always had him down for rational. He'd go to prison.
LINDA	No, he wouldn't go to prison, David. You're right – he's rational. He'd make it look like an accident. And once roused he can be incredibly jealous.
DAVID	Has he done this before? I mean . . . the accident thing?
LINDA	How would I know? Someone, a friend has an accident . . . how do I know if it's an accident or not . . . ?

(They cross and sit at a table.)

DAVID	That's true. *(Pause.)* Have many of your friends had accidents?
LINDA	One or two. Haven't yours?
DAVID	Well, yes.
LINDA	There you are then – you've nothing to worry about. I'd be more concerned about Amy. She has a suspicious nature. She's always kept a close eye on you . . . and not without cause . . .
DAVID	What do you mean – not without cause?

LINDA   I remember something she said all those
             years ago. She said: 'You're unfaithful even
             when you're being unfaithful'.

DAVID   Linda, I don't make a habit of this.

LINDA   Don't you? But that's part of the attraction.
             When I saw you for the first time in years
             on that platform . . . my heart leapt. I saw
             excitement . . . adventure . . .

DAVID   (*smirks*) Well, I've always had a devil-may-
             care attitude.

LINDA   You were leaning on a stick . . .

DAVID   Not leaning.

LINDA   I thought you were leaning quite heavily . . .

DAVID   Not heavily. I'd put my knee out playing
             squash.

LINDA   (*impressed*) Squash.

DAVID   Yes.

LINDA   So you're still quite active?

DAVID   Oh, yes. I'll let you into a little secret.
             The walking stick was more of a fashion
             statement . . .

             (*A* WAITER *enters the terrace upstage. He
             removes some glasses from a table.* DAVID
             turns sharply away.)

             My God! It's him.

LINDA   What?

DAVID   That waiter, He was here when we came the
             last time!

LINDA   David, that was years ago. He won't
             remember you. He's served thousands of
             people since then.

DAVID   I doubt that – it took him a week to serve
             me. I complained about him – don't
             you remember? I probably cost him his
             promotion – he's been waiting on tables ever
             since. Look, his feet are killing him – he can
             hardly put them to the ground . . .

             (*They watch as the* WAITER *walks painfully
             upstage and exits.*)

LINDA   Well, he's gone now. (*Leans forward.*)
             Which room?

DAVID   I'm at the back – opposite the cement works . . .

LINDA   I have a suite – with a sea view. Here's a
             key. Better this way – in case Amy checks.

DAVID   She won't – I said I'd ring her.

LINDA   She seems to have become very gullible
             over the years . . . very believing.

DAVID   It's not that she's very believing – it's more
             that she wants to believe me.

LINDA   (*considers*) I hadn't thought of it like that.
             Perhaps Robert wants to believe me?

DAVID   Look, let's have an agreement. That we
             won't talk about Robert or Amy . . .

LINDA   Agreed.

(*She leans across the table. They kiss.*
There is the flash of a camera. They freeze.
JEREMY *enters from the stairs. He has taken*
a picture of them. He is followed by CLARE
looking flushed and excited.)

CLARE   (*sees them*) Oh, would you mind taking a
             picture of us?

LINDA   Certainly.

CLARE   We're recording every moment.

LINDA   Lovely.

CLARE   And this is a special terrace where they go
             topless.

LINDA   Good heavens! I didn't know.

JEREMY   Not at night of course. (*He guffaws.*)

             (*He is moving around with his camera.*
             Looks up from the lense to see DAVID *glaring*
             at him. JEREMY *hands the camera to* LINDA.
             She takes their picture. Hands the camera
             back to JEREMY.)

JEREMY   Can I take another one of you?

DAVID   (*sharply*) No. My eyes go pink. (*Coldly.*)
             Very pink.

CLARE   Yes . . . they look quite pink now. Is this
             your first time?

LINDA   What?

CLARE   Is it your first time here?

LINDA	Oh, no. We came many years ago.
CLARE	It's an anniversary, isn't it?
LINDA	I suppose it is.
CLARE	I won't ask how long it's been.
LINDA	No, please don't.
CLARE	You see, Jeremy, love doesn't have to fade. There can still be passion.

(*She takes* JEREMY'S *hand.*)

I'll let you into a little secret. We're just married.

LINDA	I wondered if you were.
CLARE	Now we're going to walk barefoot along the beach. Isn't it romantic?

(*They exit down the steps towards the beach.* DAVID *and* LINDA *look after them in silence.*)

DAVID	What are you thinking?
LINDA	They don't look like private detectives. What are you thinking?
DAVID	How do I get hold of that camera?

(*The* WAITER *enters upstage.*)

Here's that waiter again.

LINDA	I think it's time we retired. Waiter.

(*The* WAITER *walks painfully towards them.*)

WAITER   Senora?

                (LINDA *reads his name off his badge.*)

LINDA   Carlos, could I have champagne and . . .
                some smoked salmon sandwiches sent to my
                room?

                (*She hands her key to* CARLOS *who notes the
                order.*)

CARLOS   For two, Señora?

LINDA   Yes. Si.

                (CARLOS *turns his attention to* DAVID, *who
                has retired behind one of the large menus
                lying on the table.* CARLOS' *expression
                remains impassive. He attempts to see
                beyond the menu but* DAVID *continues to
                move it between them.*)

CARLOS   (*darkly*) Just two glasses . . . ?

LINDA   Si.

                (CARLOS *and* DAVID *continue to do a dance
                with the menu.*)

CARLOS   Anything else . . . Señor?

DAVID   No. Gracias.

                (CARLOS *finally gets a good look at* DAVID.
                Their eyes meet.)

CARLOS   De nada . . .

                (CARLOS *exits painfully from the terrace.*)

DAVID	Did you see that? He recognised me.
LINDA	He didn't recognise you.
DAVID	He eyeballed me.
LINDA	He wondered why you were trying to climb inside the menu. He thought you wanted to order.
DAVID	No, he remembered me from the last time. He hasn't forgiven me. He's probably planning a phone call to England and a spot of blackmail. Why did we have to come here?
LINDA	But this is our place, David. Where our eyes first met across a crowded room.
DAVID	It's also the place where you got a cream cake in the face and my trousers ended up swinging from the bougainvillea!
LINDA	(*pats his hand*) I think it's time we retired to my room.
DAVID	Yes . . . better if we go separately . . .
LINDA	(*reproachfully*) David . . .
DAVID	Well, I've got to ring home . . . and the signal should be better here . . .
LINDA	Don't be long. I'll go by way of the garden . . . there's a smell of jasmine on the night air . . .
	(*She exits stage right by the garden path.* DAVID *blows her a kiss. Gets busy with his mobile.*)

DAVID   Hello . . . Amy?

AMY   (*voice over*) David?

DAVID   Just to let you know that I've arrived safely
           . . . I know you'd be worried . . .

AMY   I wasn't worried – if you'd crashed it would
           have been on the news. Was it a good flight?

DAVID   Yes – no turbulence.

AMY   Not yet . . .

           (AMY *enters the terrace. She is speaking
           into her mobile.*)

DAVID   I didn't catch that last remark . . . but the
           signal's incredible. We could be standing
           next to each other.

AMY   We *are* standing next to each other, David.

           (DAVID *turns and sees* AMY. *His mouth drops
           open.*)

DAVID   (*still into phone*) Amy! What are you doing
           here?

AMY   (*replies into phone*) I asked myself the
           question, was I the sort of woman who'd
           be jealous if her husband took a holiday
           without her and the answer was yes. So here
           I am. I took a week off from the shop and
           booked the next flight. (*Looks around.*) But
           where's Harry?

           (DAVID *is about to speak into the phone,
           realises, thrusts the phone into his pocket.*)

DAVID　　　　He couldn't make it . . .

AMY　　　　Couldn't?

DAVID　　　　He wasn't well.

AMY　　　　Worse than that, David.

DAVID　　　　Worse?

AMY　　　　He's dead.

DAVID　　　　Harry? He was my oldest friend. You could have broken it gently.

AMY　　　　What did you want me to say? He wasn't feeling well? I thought you knew that.

DAVID　　　　Poor old Harry. What was it?

AMY　　　　Heart.

　　　　　　(DAVID *feels his heart.*)

DAVID　　　　(*pause*) How did you know he was dead?

AMY　　　　They've buried him.

DAVID　　　　Do you have to be so flippant?

AMY　　　　Well, it couldn't have come as a surprise, David. You've been telling me for weeks that Harry was dying on his feet. Drinking half a bottle of vodka a day – still in his pyjamas until tea time. Refusing to leave the house – hanging onto the newel post if they tried to make him . . .

DAVID   I mean how did you learn he was dead?
             How did you find out? You didn't have his
             number.

AMY   I rang directory enquiries. He's been dead
             for two years, David. I don't know where
             you've been ringing him but we're going to
             have a big bill this quarter.

             (DAVID *regards her in silence*.)

DAVID   You're playing cat and mouse, aren't you?

AMY   Meeow.

DAVID   Because you don't trust me.

AMY   Of course I trust you – almost as far as I can
             throw a grand piano . . .

DAVID   Do you know how this makes me feel?

AMY   Untrusted?

DAVID   Do you know the basis of a good marriage,
             Amy – trust and understanding.

AMY   We've got that, David. You trust me and I
             understand you.

DAVID   You thought I was with a woman, didn't
             you?

AMY   Well, I knew you weren't with Harry Moffat.

DAVID   You thought I was shacked up with some
             floozy.

             (AMY *looks uneasy for the first time, even a
             little guilty*.)

AMY	I know you're not. I've checked your room – opposite the cement works – hardly a love nest.
DAVID	But you thought it.
AMY	What was I to think? All that guff about Harry Moffat who's pushing up daisies even as we speak. Why did you come here – especially to this place – one of your hunting grounds.
DAVID	It isn't one of my hunting grounds! I'm not hunting!
AMY	Then why did you come here? Why did you tell me a pack of lies?
DAVID	Because you wouldn't believe me if I told you the truth.
AMY	I would. I want to believe you, David.
DAVID	(*pause*) Well, what I told you was partly true. (*Sighs.*) Harry Moffat is here.
AMY	(*stares*) What?
DAVID	I'm Harry Moffat.
AMY	Harry Moffat – half a bottle of vodka a day – in his pyjamas until tea time – hanging onto the newel post. That Harry Moffat?
DAVID	You may not have noticed but I haven't been out of the house in weeks.
AMY	Half a bottle of vodka a day – what about the empties?

DAVID   Check under the hedge . . . down the lane.

AMY   I haven't seen you in your pyjamas – not
               during the day.

DAVID   I get changed before you get home . . .

AMY   Why?

DAVID   Because I'm finished. I should have been
               left by the roadside – that's what they do in
               some countries.

AMY   We couldn't do that, David – there's a law
               against fly-tipping.

DAVID   I knew you'd make light of it.

AMY   I'm not making light of it, David. But you're
               nothing like Harry Moffat.

DAVID   You mean, you haven't noticed. When you
               live with someone you don't always see
               the changes in them – you take them for
               granted.

AMY   What changes?

DAVID   When I say I haven't been out of the house –
               there were a couple of visits I had to make . . .

AMY   What visits?

DAVID   To my doctor . . .

AMY   (*alarmed*) What's wrong with you, David?

DAVID   That's what I asked him.

AMY   What did he say?

DAVID	He said; 'where do I start?'
AMY	As bad as that?
DAVID	Worse.
AMY	(*concerned*) What's wrong with you, David?
DAVID	I can't tell you.
AMY	Why not?
DAVID	I can't pronounce it. But it starts with the word . . . poly . . .
AMY	Poly? As in polygamy?
DAVID	(*frowns*) No, not as in polygamy. Poly means much . . . a lot . . .
AMY	A lot of what?
DAVID	(*sighs*) A lot of everything . . . except time . . .
AMY	We won't buy any green bananas then . . .
DAVID	You're not taking this seriously, Amy.
AMY	How can I? You look so well.
DAVID	That's the worst possible sign.
AMY	Is it?
DAVID	The doctor warned me about that.
AMY	How can looking well be the worst possible sign?

DAVID   Don't go by appearance. You can have a
               brightly painted front door . . . and dry rot
               in the rafters . . .

AMY   You've got dry rot as well?

DAVID   You're not listening. The doctor said beware
               of becoming dangerously flushed . . . it
               could mean you're reaching a crisis.

               (AMY *studies him.*)

AMY   You do look dangerously flushed . . . Do you
               think you're reaching a crisis?

DAVID   Who knows. Then he said something that . . .
               well, I almost laughed in his face.

AMY   That funny?

DAVID   He said, if you're going to take a holiday,
               take it now – don't wait until Christmas.

AMY   That does sound serious – but what about
               me? Don't I need a holiday?

DAVID   I told him it was out of the question – that
               you couldn't get away.

AMY   What did he say?

DAVID   He said there was no point in asking for his
               advice if I wouldn't take it. Then he added,
               it might be a good idea if you got away from
               her . . .

AMY   Away from me!

DAVID   You see, he was also worried about my
               mental condition . . .

AMY   Mental – ! (*Stares.*) There is a lot wrong
            with you, isn't there, David?

DAVID   He's my doctor – I have no secrets from
            him.

AMY   Then he's the only one.

DAVID   He knows all about my sense of failure – my
            jealousy . . .

AMY   Jealousy? What jealousy?

DAVID   Of you and Aubrey.

AMY   (*stares*) Aubrey Broadbent?

DAVID   The butcher.

AMY   What have you got to be jealous about?

DAVID   You spend a lot of time in that shop, . . .

AMY   David, it's freezing in there.

DAVID   So what? He's used to it. He's at his best at
            low temperatures.

AMY   He may be, but I'm not.

DAVID   I wouldn't blame you, Amy. I've not been
            good to you.

AMY   No, you haven't.

DAVID   You deserve better . . . a chance for
            happiness.

AMY   I don't want happiness – I want you, David.

DAVID	I can't afford sirloin steak, Amy. That's why I told you that story about Harry Moffat. To give you that chance . . . and if I don't make it through these few days . . . well, I know you'll be taken care of . . .
AMY	I don't want to be taken care of.
DAVID	I thought it would give you the chance to find out what you do want.
AMY	I know what I want. That's why I'm here and not with Aubrey. And I've told the people at reception that I'm moving in with you . . .
DAVID	Moving in?
AMY	Yes, and you know the effect hotel bedrooms have on me . . . remember our honeymoon . . . when we broke the leg off the bed.
DAVID	I remember.
AMY	Well, this can be our second honeymoon – no, third I was forgetting that regrettable incident that took place at this very hotel all those years ago. Remember?
DAVID	I remember.
AMY	You'll observe I haven't mentioned that regrettable incident?
DAVID	I have observed that.
AMY	Or that awful woman.
DAVID	Was she? I don't remember . . .

(AMY *puts her arms around him.*)

AMY	I promise you'll forget everything when I get you in there . . .
DAVID	You go.
AMY	What?
DAVID	I have to take a stroll before bed. Doctor's orders.
AMY	Why?
DAVID	To encourage my endorphins.
AMY	Endorphins? What are they?
DAVID	They're sort of hormones.
AMY	Hormones. (*Grins.*) I'm all for that, David.
DAVID	It helps to kill the pain.
AMY	Do you have much pain?
DAVID	It's creeping – it's a sort of creeping illness.
AMY	As long as it doesn't creep too far.
DAVID	Arthritic in origin.
AMY	Arthritic. Something that surprises me, David.
DAVID	What?
AMY	You didn't bring your walking stick . . .
DAVID	I'm trying to do without it.

(*She studies him for a moment.*)

AMY   I brought it – just in case. (*Pause.*)
           Creeping?

DAVID   Yes.

AMY   That sounds like you.

DAVID   What?

AMY   (*anxiously*) Still, not life threatening?

DAVID   (*sighs*) Who knows?

AMY   Well, before you go for your walk . . . I'm
           feeling romantic . . . let's have a last look at
           the stars . . .

           (AMY *leads* DAVID *off upstage.* CLARE *and*
           JEREMY *enter from the beach.*)

CLARE   (*giggling and looking back*) Everyone seems
           to know we're newly-weds.

JEREMY   That's because you keep telling them.

CLARE   You don't think it shows?

JEREMY   What?

CLARE   That I'm a young bride?

JEREMY   Well, hardly young . . .

CLARE   What?

JEREMY   The cake has lost a little of its icing . . .

CLARE   Icing! Is that how you feel?

JEREMY	Clare, you can't doubt my feelings. You've been putting it off for years. I've always wanted to get married.
CLARE	I know. I discovered that at the reception.
JEREMY	What did you discover?
CLARE	That you'd proposed to three other women before me.
JEREMY	(*uneasily*) That was ages ago.
CLARE	Even so, Jeremy. Three women – and two on the same night.
JEREMY	I was in a hurry.
CLARE	So it would appear.
JEREMY	Clare, I'm a serving officer. Can you blame me for wanting to seize the moment?
CLARE	There's a difference between seizing the moment and making a grab at it. (*Pause.*) Don't pull a face, Jeremy. I know I've delayed but there were reasons. I had to be sure. And then there was father . . .
JEREMY	What about him?
CLARE	I had to wait for him to pass on . . .
JEREMY	Pass on? Why?
CLARE	He couldn't stand you.
JEREMY	I didn't know that. Why couldn't he stand me?

CLARE   He said he found you repellent. So I thought
               I'd better wait. At least he didn't die of a
               heart attack.

JEREMY   Good heavens! Now I suppose he's turning
               in his grave.

CLARE   He would be – if he hadn't been cremated.
               But never mind, Jeremy. We're married now.
               And I'm blissfully happy. Aren't you?

JEREMY   Yes – blissfully.

CLARE   It's just that marriage shouldn't be entered
               into lightly – it's a serious undertaking. I
               had to say to myself can I look at that face
               over the marmalade for the rest of my life.

JEREMY   I don't like marmalade.

CLARE   You see – we're still finding things out
               about each other. I don't want any nasty
               surprises. I want this to last. Too many
               people marry in haste and repent at leisure.
               I want us to be like that couple we've just
               met. Still in love after all those years – still
               passionate about each other . . .

               (CLARE's *voice dies away as* AMY *and* DAVID
               return to the terrace hand in hand.)

AMY   Well, go for your walk . . .

               (*She embraces him.*)

               And hurry. I can't wait to get you into bed . . .

               (CLARE's *mouth drops open.* AMY *sees* CLARE
               for the first time and smiles politely.)

CLARE

Well. Really!

(She sweeps off, followed by JEREMY. AMY *looks at* DAVID *for an explanation.)*

DAVID

(shrugs) Newly-weds.

(He moves off as if this explains it. AMY *follows looking puzzled. The light comes up on the balcony.* LINDA *appears through the French windows. She leans over the balcony and sighs.)*

LINDA

'On such a night as this' . . .

(Hears a sound at the door.)

Come in. It's open. Know what this reminds me of? 'Private Lives'. All I need is a white Molyneux dress . . .

*(*ROBERT *appears through the French doors and stands behind* LINDA. *He slides his arms around her waist.)*

Have you missed me already?

ROBERT

What do you think?

(Something in the voice checks LINDA. *She puts her hand behind her and feels* ROBERT'S *face. She finds his moustache. She turns and almost falls into his arms.)*

LINDA

Robert.

ROBERT

Linda, you've gone limp – what is it?

LINDA

The excitement of seeing you again.

ROBERT   Good Lord! It's only been a few days. I must
              go away more often.

LINDA   Yes . . .

ROBERT   I'm famished – been travelling all day. I'll
              ring room service. What would you like?

              (*He's moving through the French door.*)

LINDA   (*quickly*) Smoked salmon sandwiches and
              champagne. But the service is appalling. I
              think we'll move on in the morning . . .

              (ROBERT *pops his head back.*)

ROBERT   That's because you're a woman travelling
              alone. You'll see a difference now . . . .

              (*He disappears.*)

LINDA   I'm sure I shall.

ROBERT   (*voice off*) Room service? Champagne and
              salmon sandwiches for two . . . 301. Oh, and
              I've heard complaints about the service so
              make it snappy . . .

              (ROBERT *returns to the balcony.*)

              That should do the trick . . .

LINDA   You're so masterful, Robert.

              (CARLOS *emerges through the French doors.
              He is carrying a tray bearing champagne
              and sandwiches.*)

ROBERT   What the . . . ! How did they . . . ?

(CARLOS *assembles the food and turns. He sees* ROBERT *for the first time and does a double take.* ROBERT, *still looking puzzled, signs the pad.* CARLOS *exits.* ROBERT *stares after him and back at* LINDA.)

ROBERT   That was quick. How did they do that?

LINDA   (*thinking quickly*) I ordered them before you came.

ROBERT   Then you got my message?

LINDA   (*relieved*) Yes, dear.

ROBERT   Only you seemed surprised to see me. You sort of lurched . . .

LINDA   My heart often lurches when I haven't seen you for a while, Robert. But weren't you supposed to be in Rome?

ROBERT   We've been taken over.

LINDA   By the Italians. Isn't that why you went to Rome?

ROBERT   Yes, but they were taken over by the Swedes.

LINDA   So it's off to Sweden.

ROBERT   No, they were taken over by the Germans – who have eventually succumbed to the Japanese. And that's it. We've been taken over by the three Axis powers and a neutral . . .

LINDA   (*sighs*) Not the war, Robert.

ROBERT   I sometimes wonder who won it. I knew
              we were in trouble when I saw that the new
              chairman was five foot two and mustard
              coloured. He gave us a severe lecture – I'm
              sure he shouted 'tenko'. Then he sent us
              home to consult our ancestors. If we don't
              come up with the goods it's a long knife and
              a prayer mat for yours truly. (*He takes a
              sandwich.*) These sandwiches are delicious.

              (LINDA *looks anxiously out over balcony.*)

LINDA   Not yet, Robert. Have your shower first . . . .

              (*She begins to usher him back into the
              room.*)

ROBERT   (*pause*) We've been here before, haven't we?

LINDA   What?

ROBERT   I recognised the waiter – very bad on his
              feet.

LINDA   Yes . . . we have been here . . . years ago.

ROBERT   Now I remember . . .

LINDA   (*anxiously*) Yes?

ROBERT   Our plumbing was a disgrace . . . we had to
              use a Frenchman's lavatory.

LINDA   It hasn't got any better. A man on the next
              floor found his bath full of effluent.

ROBERT   Effluent! My God! We'll check out in the
              morning.

LINDA	We'll go to the Alhambra. That's much nicer.

(She finally gets ROBERT *off the balcony. Voices off.)*

ROBERT	Watch those jets, Linda. Don't want to get covered in crap.

(Sound of shower. LINDA *reappears and snatches up a towel. She looks anxiously out over balcony.)*

ROBERT	*(off)* Linda.
LINDA	Coming . . .

(She hurries back to bathroom. Sound of door closing. A moment later, DAVID *enters the balcony. He notes the sound of the shower. He takes a sandwich and chews it pensively.* LINDA *enters in a panic. The rest of the scene is played out like an old silent film melodrama with exaggerated lips and hand movements. No speech.)*

LINDA	*(mimes)* Robert's here!
DAVID	*(mimes)* What?
LINDA	Robert.
DAVID	Who?
LINDA	Robert!

(She opens and closes her hands.)

DAVID	Robert!

(*He glances in alarm towards bathroom.*)

My God! That's not all.

LINDA   What isn't?

DAVID   Amy's here.

(LINDA *studies his lips.*)

LINDA   Who's here?

DAVID   Amy!

(*He mimes pushing a pie in* LINDA's *face.*)

LINDA   Amy! What are we going to do? She'll kill me.

DAVID   He'll kill me!

(*Sound of* ROBERT *approaching.*)

ROBERT   (*off*) I really must have another sandwich before I shower . . .

(LINDA *makes a 'leave, get away' motion with her hands.* DAVID *looks at her then over the balcony and back again, in horror.* LINDA *is still waving him away.* ROBERT *enters.* DAVID *disappears over the balcony.* ROBERT *picks up a sandwich. He looks out into the night.*)

ROBERT   Did you hear a cry?

LINDA   No.

ROBERT   Thought I heard a cry.

LINDA   Probably an owl . . .

                (*She follows* ROBERT *back into the room. She closes the French window. Silence.*)

DAVID   (*off, faintly, a plaintive wail*) Help . . .

                (*Curtain.*)

Scene Two

Hotel. Mid morning. The terrace is deserted.

LINDA *is alone on the balcony. She is wearing a large sun hat with a broad brim tilted over her face and dark glasses. She is studying the effect in a hand mirror. The effect is both inscrutable and anonymous.*

ROBERT *enters. He is wearing blazer and flannels and a cravat and has clearly been for a brisk walk.*

ROBERT   You look mysterious.

LINDA   Do I? I thought I'd cover up today – they say it's going to be hot. Did you arrange the transfer?

ROBERT   No problem. The Alhambra is their sister hotel so they can move us later in the day. And it can't come soon enough . . .

LINDA   (*uneasily*) Why do you say that, Robert?

ROBERT   It's this place. It sort of brought it all back.

LINDA   Brought all what back?

ROBERT   I think you know what I mean.

LINDA   No, I don't, Robert.

ROBERT   This is where you met that man who caused
             all the trouble, who tried to come between
             us, who wouldn't leave you alone.

LINDA   You mean the man you threatened to kill,
             that man?

ROBERT   And I meant it. I said if he ever came near
             you again . . .

LINDA   Robert, that was years ago.

ROBERT   One doesn't forget a thing like that, and this
             place is bringing it all back. What was his
             name . . . ?

LINDA   I don't remember.

ROBERT   David. That was it. He must have been
             preying on my mind because I thought I saw
             him.

LINDA   What! Where?

ROBERT   Coming out of the hotel. Of course it wasn't
             him but . . .

LINDA   But what?

ROBERT   Well, his hair was grey, and his head was on
             one side . . . one arm seemed shorter than
             the other . . . and he had a pronounced limp
             . . . but apart from that . . .

LINDA   Apart from that! There's nothing left.

ROBERT   Apart from that – it was just like him.

LINDA	Robert, you can't say that a man with his head on one side, one arm shorter than the other, and a pronounced limp is just like someone whose head isn't on one side, has both arms the same length and doesn't have a limp, can you?
ROBERT	I suppose you're right.

(LINDA *observes his hands opening and closing.*)

	I had one of my dreams last night. He was in it.
LINDA	One of your dreams. Don't tell me about it. I don't like your dreams, Robert. They're not very nice.
ROBERT	I haven't had this one for a long time.
LINDA	Perhaps, but I'm sure you were in some public place, in your pyjamas, looking for a loo.
ROBERT	I wasn't in my pyjamas.
LINDA	But you were looking for a loo and you couldn't find one, or it was occupied, or there wasn't a door on it, or there were three people trying to get in at the same time. It's an insecurity dream, Robert. You're dreadfully insecure.
ROBERT	I wasn't looking for a loo. That wasn't what the dream was about. I was getting an ice cream cornet from the kiosk by the pool . . .
LINDA	Were you in your pyjamas?

ROBERT	No! (*Pause.*) Although I did appear to have mislaid my trousers. As I was getting the cornet . . . this chap comes along . . . David. He gets one too.
LINDA	Was he in his pyjamas?
ROBERT	No!
LINDA	Or without his trousers?
ROBERT	He was fully clothed.
LINDA	You see?
ROBERT	What do you mean – you see?
LINDA	He's not insecure.
ROBERT	Linda, it wasn't his dream. It was mine. How do you know what he's like in his dreams? He could be totally naked.
LINDA	Only if he was insecure.
ROBERT	As I was saying. We both bought cornets and we ran back to you with them.
LINDA	Me?
ROBERT	Yes. And we offered you our cornets . . .
LINDA	Was I in pyjamas?
ROBERT	No! Will you stop talking about pyjamas?
LINDA	I'm sorry, but does this dream have any point?

ROBERT   I'm coming to it. We offered you our cornets
                and you accepted . . . David's . . .

LINDA   I accepted David's cornet?

ROBERT   Yes.

LINDA   Were you upset?

ROBERT   At first but then I looked down and saw that
                my cornet had melted . . .

LINDA   Oh dear. I can see how disturbing that must
                have been.

ROBERT   It was.

LINDA   Standing there without your trousers then
                looking down and finding that your cornet
                had melted.

ROBERT   Right. And that's why I shall be happy
                to leave this place. Too many painful
                memories.

                (*He turns to go back through the French
                windows.*)

                And I'm not the only one who finds this
                hotel oppressive. A guest tried to kill
                himself last night . . .

LINDA   What was that, Robert?

ROBERT   They were talking about it in reception.
                Well, that's what they thought. Went so
                far with it then changed his mind – lost
                his nerve, I suppose. He said he'd tripped
                but no one believed him. He was hanging
                from one of the balconies. They had to use

an extendable ladder to get him down. It
must have happened whilst we were in the
bathroom – so we missed all the excitement,.
It was somewhere near here . . .

(ROBERT *exits*.)

LINDA   (*worried frown*) Somewhere near here . . . ?
                    Robert . . .

                    (LINDA *follows*. CLARE *is sitting at a table on
                    the terrace*. JEREMY *enters breezily*.)

JEREMY   I've got tickets for the trip . . .

CLARE   Good.

                    (*He studies her serious expression*.)

JEREMY   Sorry I took so long but they were all
                    talking about the suicide attempt.

CLARE   What suicide attempt?

JEREMY   A chap tried to kill himself only he landed
                    on another balcony – then, apparently, he
                    lost his nerve. They say he hung there until
                    his arms were nearly out of their sockets.
                    They're still trying to find him.

CLARE   Why?

JEREMY   Frightened he might try it again. The trouble
                    is they're not sure what he looks like. He ran
                    off into the darkness.

CLARE   A man?

JEREMY   Yes – why?

CLARE	At least it wasn't that poor woman.
JEREMY	Yes, that was a shock.
CLARE	They seemed so happy together . . . and then . . . that. It does make one wonder.
JEREMY	They had been married a long time.
CLARE	We wouldn't be like that, would we, Jeremy?
JEREMY	Of course not, darling . . . Although I suppose marriage can become dulled by daily routine . . .
CLARE	Yes . . . (*Pause.*) Do you gargle every morning?
JEREMY	Yes. Do you mind?
CLARE	No, only it was so unexpected – I thought you were unblocking the hand basin.
JEREMY	I suppose we're going to surprise each other. I was surprised to see the curlers.
CLARE	Only briefly, Jeremy. The sea air does flatten my hair rather . . . You don't mind?
JEREMY	No – you just looked different. It was the first time I'd actually seen your forehead.
CLARE	(*concerned*) There's nothing wrong with it, is there?
JEREMY	Of course not.
CLARE	You must tell me. I intend to keep our marriage alive . . . not like that poor woman . . . oh. (*Lowers voice.*) Here she is . . .

(LINDA *enters terrace from the path. She is
still in dark glasses and low brimmed hat
together with robe, collar turned up. She
looks about cautiously.*)

JEREMY   (*lowers voice*) Dark glasses . . .

CLARE   Eyes red from weeping, I'd imagine. I must
                talk to her.

JEREMY   It's not really our business, Clare.

CLARE   It's the business of every woman, Jeremy . . .

                (CLARE *rises and crosses to where* LINDA
                *is standing looking uncertainly down the
                steps to the beach. She taps* LINDA *on the
                shoulder.* LINDA *turns with a start.*)

CLARE   I just want to say . . .

LINDA   Yes?

CLARE   (*solemnly*) Don't give up.

LINDA   (*nervously*) I won't.

CLARE   You're still a beautiful woman.

LINDA   (*politely*) Thank you.

CLARE   I've seen the way he looked at you and I saw
                the way he looked at her. He still loves you.

LINDA   Good. That's . . . er . . . nice to know.

CLARE   Don't let a cheap infatuation spoil all that . . .
                don't let her come between you. Fight.

                (LINDA *is trying to move off.*)

LINDA   I will.

CLARE   You're not ugly.

LINDA   I'm not. Oh, good.

CLARE   Don't let her make you feel you are.

LINDA   I won't. Well, I must get on . . .

               (LINDA *turns towards the steps then turns
               back abruptly, crosses upstage and settles
               on a far sun lounger.* CLARE *sees who's
               coming up the steps and returns to her
               table.* AMY *enters from the steps.*)

AMY   Come on, David – plenty of room up here . . .

               (DAVID *enters slowly. He is leaning on a
               stick. His head is on one side and he's
               limping. He looks considerably misshapen.
               He is wearing dark glasses.*)

CLARE   (*stares*) My God! (*Whispers.*) Look at him.
               Look at the difference from last night.
               What's she done to him? She must be an
               animal . . .

JEREMY   (*anxiously*) Keep your voice down, Clare.
               It's really none of our business . . .

CLARE   You're right. And I can't bear to watch them.
               We'll go on the beach.

               (CLARE *rises, glares at* AMY *and exits,
               followed by* JEREMY.)

AMY   (*stares after* CLARE) Why does she always
               scowl at me?

DAVID   I've no idea. Perhaps you're the sort of person people scowl at.

AMY   There's no need to be grumpy just because you're in pain. Let's sit over here . . .

        (*They cross to a table downstage.* DAVID *sits with difficulty. She studies him.*)

        That creeping thing seems to have crept a bit more.

DAVID   (*sighs*) I know.

AMY   I wouldn't know you.

DAVID   You wouldn't?

        (*He looks hopeful.*)

AMY   You were hopeless last night. That room isn't doing us any good. I woke up this morning covered in cement dust.

DAVID   (*nods*) I think they were working a double shift.

AMY   I went to reception to see if I could get an upgrade.

DAVID   Did you?

AMY   (*shakes head*) They were too busy talking about the suicide attempt.

DAVID   What suicide attempt?

AMY   This man, obviously having a bad time, decided to end it all, then lost his nerve. They're trying to track him down.

DAVID   (*nervously*) Why do they want to do that?

AMY   Why? In case he tries it again. They don't
        want him dropping on people – and then
        there's the mess – takes a lot of cleaning up
        – it's like strawberry jam.

DAVID   I don't suppose he'll try it again.

AMY   You never know with these people. The
        trouble is they haven't got a very good
        description. He ran off before they could get
        his particulars. They said he ran in a funny
        way . . . dragging his leg, head on one side
        . . . Of course that may be the trouble – he
        may be fed up with his body . . . bit like you.

DAVID   I'm not fed up with my body.

AMY   It wasn't much use to you last night – it
        wasn't much use to me either. I suppose it's
        taking its revenge.

DAVID   (*stares*) Revenge? Revenge for what?

AMY   All those years . . .

DAVID   All those years of what?

AMY   Abuse.

DAVID   I haven't abused my body.

AMY   You haven't? Then it must have been mine.

DAVID   What's the matter, Amy – you're in a mood.

AMY   I was disappointed. Those endorphins
        haven't done the trick. I arrived here with
        all sorts of romantic notions – just like that

girl who went down the steps. She arrived
in reception yesterday all smiles, I saw her.
Now she's full of doom and gloom.

DAVID She's probably been disappointed. She
probably had high expectations – and it's not
like that.

AMY It isn't?

DAVID No, she's had to come down to earth . . .
make adjustments.

AMY (*pause*) Did you make adjustments?

DAVID What?

AMY Did you make adjustments – on our
honeymoon?

DAVID Well, yes. What you expect and what you
get, well . . .

AMY Well, what?

DAVID Nothing's perfect.

AMY It certainly wasn't.

DAVID There you are then. (*Pause.*) Wasn't what?

AMY Perfect.

DAVID Right.

AMY I had a few shocks . . .

DAVID Shocks?

AMY Yes.

DAVID   What sort of shocks?

AMY   (*shakes head*) That first night . . .

DAVID   What about that first night?

AMY   After I'd given my all . . .

DAVID   Your all! What about my all?

AMY   After I'd given my all. I lay there trying
             to get to sleep when I heard this gnawing
             sound. It was like sleeping next to a
             hamster. I switched on the light and found
             you eating a Cornish pasty.

DAVID   I was hungry. I often got hungry in the
             night.

AMY   You should have controlled it. I was half the
             night getting the crumbs out of the bed. It
             was disgusting.

David   Disgusting! If I'm so disgusting why did you
             ask me to marry you?

AMY   I didn't.

DAVID   Perhaps you've forgotten.

AMY   I haven't forgotten anything.

DAVID   You don't remember that you proposed.

AMY   Proposed! Women don't propose.

DAVID   You did.

AMY   You said you loved me.

DAVID   That's not a proposal.

AMY   I didn't propose.

DAVID   You did.

AMY   What did I do – go down on one knee?

DAVID   No – you were flat on your back at the time.

AMY   What! Flat on my back?

DAVID   Yes. It was after our first time.

AMY   I remember that. I didn't propose.

DAVID   You did.

AMY   What did I say?

DAVID   You said, 'When do we get the ring?' The next day I found myself in Bravingtons.

AMY   That wasn't a proposal. That was merely an enquiry. I'm hungry. Let's have some coffee and cake . . .

             (DAVID *sighs and signals to* CARLOS *who has entered the terrace. He crosses painfully.*)

CARLOS   Señor?

DAVID   Coffee, por favor.

AMY   And some cream cakes . . .

             (CARLOS *turns to* AMY, *seeing her for the first time. He does a double take. Recovers and bows.*)

Señor . . .

(*He walks away.*)

AMY	Why does everyone stare at me?
DAVID	I thought you'd be used to it by now.
AMY	No – there's something strange going on. It's because I'm with you.
DAVID	It is not. There's nothing strange about me.
AMY	Perhaps they think I'm being kept. After all, you look so much older. That young couple didn't seem to approve. Very poker-faced. And she was laughing when they arrived.
DAVID	Well, he is rather pompous. He has no sense of humour. That's a vital ingredient.
AMY	Vital ingredient?
DAVID	In a marriage.
AMY	Why haven't we got it?
DAVID	We have. I have a very keen sense of humour. I make people laugh.
AMY	Not intentionally.
DAVID	I have a very well developed sense of humour, whereas you haven't. It isn't your fault. You have to be born with it. Few women have a sense of humour.
AMY	That's because they have nothing to laugh about.

DAVID   You see – how bitter you sound. That's why
          you haven't a sense of humour.

AMY   And you have?

DAVID   Yes.

AMY   David, anyone who thinks musical
          underpants is the pinnacle of wit can hardly
          claim to have a keen sense of humour.

DAVID   They were a gift. I didn't buy them.

AMY   You wore them. And all over Christmas
          we had 'Jingle Bells' coming out of your
          trousers.

DAVID   Everyone thought it was funny.

AMY   Not Christmas morning in church when we
          had 'Jingle Bells' competing with 'Come All
          Ye Faithful'.

DAVID   I couldn't always control it.

AMY   I noticed that when you were flirting with
          that woman from the garage.

DAVID   I wasn't flirting.

AMY   Your underpants were . . .

          (CARLOS *arrives with coffee and cakes.*)

AMY   Any cake?

DAVID   No.

AMY   Goody. More for me.

(She has the cake half way to her lips when she spots LINDA *who is seizing the opportunity to leave the terrace. The cake remains half way to* AMY's *mouth as* LINDA *passes the table. Their eyes meet.)*

LINDA   *(smiles)* Bonjour.

(She exits down the steps watched narrowly by AMY.)

DAVID   *(uneasily)* French.

AMY   She's not French.

DAVID   Oh, perhaps she thought you were French.

AMY   No – she knew me. Didn't you recognise her?

DAVID   *(innocently)* Do we know her?

AMY   I'd know that walk anywhere – even after all these years. That's one thing you can't change – the walk.

DAVID   What sort of walk?

AMY   She always walked as if people were watching her – even when they weren't.

DAVID   How do you know?

AMY   I've watched her.

DAVID   Then she was being watched . . . when she thought she was being watched.

AMY   But she didn't know she was being watched.

DAVID   She did just now – your eyes were boring
             into her.

             (AMY *regards* DAVID *suspiciously.*)

AMY   You don't know who she is?

DAVID   No.

AMY   Then why are you defending her.

DAVID   I'm not. She's nothing to me. Who is she?

AMY   Cast your mind back a few years . . . We
             met her here at this very hotel and she made
             quite an impression on you . . .

             (DAVID *looks after* LINDA. *Shakes head.*)

DAVID   No . . . The woman of whom you speak,
             whose name evades me at the moment,
             was much older. She's probably in an old
             people's home by now.

AMY   Old people's home! She was years younger
             than you. Most people are. In fact I don't
             know anyone older than you – not since
             mother died. You're old – you're the oldest
             person in this hotel.

DAVID   (*looks around, appalled*) What about the
             waiter.

AMY   I wasn't counting the staff.

DAVID   Well, what about him?

AMY   He could be your son.

DAVID   I am not old.

AMY

Well, you look it. Although I must say you didn't look old when I arrived last night . . . But then you didn't come here to die, did you? You came here to mess around. One last fling before they screwed you down. You only aged when I arrived.

DAVID

Well, you can be very ageing. And I wasn't messing around. I'm a sick man.

AMY

You're a hypochondriac – always have been.

DAVID

Perhaps but now I'm a sick hypochondriac. And if that woman of whom you speak whose name evades me at the moment –

AMY

Linda! She's the 'woman of whom I speak'. I can always tell when you're lying – you get very formal.

DAVID

I'm not lying. I only wish there was a bible here.

AMY

That's just like you. You'd commit sacrilege to get out of a situation.

DAVID

This is not a situation.

(AMY *stands menacingly.*)

AMY

David, if you don't think this is a situation I have a surprise for you . . .

(DAVID *holds out his walking stick in a fencing gesture.*)

DAVID

Now, Amy, stand back. The ferrule on the end of this stick is quite sharp . . . I wouldn't want to hurt you . . .

(AMY *subsides for a moment and sits.*)

If this woman is here, which I doubt, it's
pure chance.

AMY   Pure chance. They all knew. That's why I've
                been getting these strange looks. They all
                know more than me.

DAVID   Well, that's not surprising – you left school
                at fifteen and you've hardly read a book
                since.

AMY   That's typical – to throw my lack of
                education in my face. You've never let me
                forget that I failed my eleven-plus. You've
                no idea how that scars a person. I suppose
                she's highly educated – the sort who can
                speak a dozen languages and can't say no in
                any of them.

DAVID   I wouldn't know. As far as I'm aware that
                woman is a stranger to me . . . and if she
                isn't then it's a complete coincidence.

AMY   I don't believe in coincidence, David – not
                where you're concerned.

DAVID   It can happen. Remember when we went
                on that trip to Madam Tussauds? Who was
                the first person we saw in the Chamber of
                Horrors? Your mother.

AMY   Don't try and relieve this situation by being
                funny, David.

DAVID   I'm not. I'm merely pointing out that life's
                full of coincidences. What about Weymouth
                last year? You paddled next to a girl whose

father turned out to be the cousin of the man
who repaired our TV set.

AMY   I do not call that a coincidence. The
chances of meeting Linda here, after all
these years . . .

DAVID   That's what makes it a coincidence. I knew
a man who went fishing and found his
grandmother's wedding ring in sixty foot of
water.

AMY   That doesn't surprise me. She probably
threw it there. I'm sure you'll find plenty of
wedding rings in sixty foot of water. One
day they'll find mine – the difference is –
I'll be wearing it.

                    (AMY *stands again. She picks up a cream
                    cake.*)

DAVID   Now, Amy keep calm.

AMY   I wondered why you wanted to go on holiday
with a man who'd been dead for two years.
I mean it's not every one's idea of a good
time.

                    (*She balances the cake in her hand.*)

DAVID   Amy, don't start throwing things. You're not
at home now.

AMY   I feel like throwing things.

                    (DAVID *darts a glance at* CARLOS *who is
                    standing by in a disapproving attitude but
                    pretending not to listen.*)

DAVID   (*hisses*) We'll be asked to leave.

AMY   I don't care.

                (*She throws the cake. It misses* DAVID *and
                strikes* CARLOS *on the jacket.* CARLOS *stares
                down at the creamy mess in monumental
                horror.*)

DAVID   Now look what you've done.

AMY   You shouldn't have moved.

DAVID   (*smiles apologetically*) I'll pay for the dry
                cleaning . . .

                (CARLOS *turns haughtily on his heels and
                exits.* AMY *slumps into her chair.*)

DAVID   See. You've offended him. He'll be spitting
                in the soup now. That's if he bothers to
                serve us. And all for nothing. If the woman
                of whom you speak is here . . .

AMY   You know she's here. This was a tryst.

DAVID   A what?

AMY   A tryst.

DAVID   What's that?

AMY   A romantic meeting between lovers. Not
                bad for someone who didn't pass her eleven-
                plus.

DAVID   It wasn't a tryst.

AMY   An assignation.

DAVID   I have not been assignating.

AMY	A dirty weekend.
DAVID	Amy, my idea of a dirty weekend is clearing out the coal-shed. If that woman of whom you speak is here . . .
AMY	Linda.
DAVID	She's probably here with her husband. All right – we met them here years ago. For all we know they come here every year.
AMY	She didn't come here with her husband. This was a tryst.
DAVID	Don't keep saying that.
AMY	Well don't keep saying the woman of whom you speak. Her name is Linda – as you well know – her husband's name is Robert. And he's not here. You wouldn't be here if he was because he threatened to duff you up.
DAVID	You don't think he's here? You think I'm afraid of him?
AMY	David, if Robert's here with Linda . . . I'll eat that bowl of flowers . . .
DAVID	All of them?
AMY	Yes, stems and all.
DAVID	You may regret that, Amy,
AMY	(*emotionally*) The only thing I regret is marrying you.

(*She chokes back a sob. She rises and crosses to the stairs.* ROBERT *enters from the*

stairs. He fails to notice AMY, *since her nose
is buried in a handkerchief.*)

DAVID   Amy!

(*He slips on his dark glasses. He follows.
He fails to be aware of* ROBERT *until he's
confronted by him. They try to move out of
each other's way but fail.* ROBERT *regards
him closely.* DAVID *ensures that his dark
glasses are on securely. He begins to use his
stick as a blind man would. He taps around*
ROBERT *and then begins to tap* ROBERT *as if
establishing his height and weight.* ROBERT'S
*expression remains impassive, he takes hold
of the end of the stick.*)

DAVID   Ah. Guten Morgen.

ROBERT   Oh. (*Hesitates.*) Er, guten Morgen . . .

(ROBERT *passes on and exits.* DAVID *breathes
a sigh of relief and collapses into a chair.*
AMY *returns to him, her eyes wide open.*)

AMY   (*sits*) That was Robert.

DAVID   I know.

AMY   Then you remember him?

DAVID   You don't forget someone who's threatened
               to kill you.

AMY   Is that why you pretended to be German?

DAVID   Yes, Robert never had any time for the
               Germans. So I thought a German tourist . . .

AMY   A blind German tourist . . .

DAVID	Not blind – partially sighted. I'm not mocking the blind.
AMY	Still, it was very disarming. You wouldn't be climbing any balconies in that state . . .

(DAVID *pretends to be amused.*)

DAVID	(*laughs*) Indeed not.
AMY	That was quick thinking, David.
DAVID	It had to be. Thank God I've always been able to think on my feet.
AMY	I have noticed that . . . (*Pause.*) I feel so ashamed.
DAVID	Why?
AMY	I didn't believe you. I thought you'd come here to meet Linda.
DAVID	(*generously*) It was an honest mistake.
AMY	No, it wasn't. I'm a suspicious and jealous woman. I never give you the benefit of the doubt.
DAVID	(*nods*) You should watch that, Amy.
AMY	I will, I will in future. Say you forgive me, David.
DAVID	(*magnanimously*) There's nothing to forgive.
AMY	There is – there's everything to forgive.
DAVID	It can sour a relationship . . .

AMY   Don't say that, David. How was I to know
               Robert was here? If I'd known that . . . You
               wouldn't have arranged to meet Linda with
               Robert in tow – not with the chance of being
               hurled from a balcony. You're too big a
               coward for that . . .

DAVID   (*stares*) Well, that's one way of looking at
               it. Or it could be that I have some scruples
               left – that I have too much regard for you
               to embark on an affair with this woman . . .
               whose name evades me at the moment.

AMY   Linda.

DAVID   Linda.

AMY   Say you forgive me, David.

DAVID   Of course I forgive you.

AMY   (*starting to rise*) I'll order some lunch.

DAVID   (*quietly*) Aren't you forgetting something?

               (*He takes a bowl of flowers from an
               adjacent table and places them in front of
               AMY. He takes up the cruet and begins to
               salt and pepper the flowers.*)

               (*Curtain. End of Act One.*)

ACT TWO

Scene One

Hotel. Mid afternoon.

The terrace is deserted.

LINDA *is alone on the balcony. She is waving to someone below. First there are 'stay away' signs followed by a thumb pointing behind her.*

ROBERT *appears at the entrance to the balcony. He regards her curiously.*

ROBERT	Are you waving to someone?
LINDA	(*stares*) Yes . . . that nice young couple . . . just married . . . first time here. So sweet.
ROBERT	Are they?
LINDA	You don't think so?
ROBERT	He gave me a very dark look as I was coming from reception. I don't think things are working out.
LINDA	Well, they have to get used to each other. Look how long it took for me to get used to you . . .
ROBERT	Yes . . .
LINDA	(*hastily*) And how well it worked out.
ROBERT	(*pause*) They said a funny thing at reception . . .
LINDA	Funny? What was that? Amuse me.

ROBERT   They apologised for not passing on my
                message – to say I was coming. I said they
                must have done. You had everything ready . . .

LINDA   Of course they must have done – they've
                probably forgotten.

ROBERT   That's what I said . . . but they were
                adamant . . .

LINDA   Well, they're wrong – (*Stops.*) Unless . . .
                and this is almost mystical, Robert.

ROBERT   Mystical?

LINDA   That I sensed your coming. We do have this
                affinity . . . this uncanny understanding . . .
                almost a sixth sense. Something that young
                couples have to learn.

ROBERT   I think they've probably had too much sun.
                Not used to it. Twenty minutes the first day
                – that's what I always say.

LINDA   It is hot. Do you mind checking the
                Alhambra on your own? I'm fagged.

ROBERT   No – better if I deal with them I know these
                people. I'll make sure we get a decent room.
                What will you do?

LINDA   Just sun myself . . .

ROBERT   By the way, someone took a picture of that
                man. They were showing it around the
                lobby.

LINDA   What man?

ROBERT   The man who tried to commit suicide. They
            took it as he was running away. Not a very
            good picture but it's all they've got to go on.

LINDA   Oh, that man.

ROBERT   And do you know who he reminded me of . . . ?

LINDA   I know what you're going to say. He
            reminded you of this man with his head on
            one side, who reminds you of this man we
            met years ago – whose name I've forgotten.

ROBERT   (*frowns, considers*) No, he reminded me of
            this blind German.

LINDA   (*stares*) Blind German? What blind German?

ROBERT   I met him this morning. Well, when I say
            met him I almost bumped into him. Come to
            think of it, he reminded me of the man with
            his head on one side . . .

LINDA   (*accusingly*) And who did the man with his
            head on one side remind you of, Robert?

ROBERT   You know who.

LINDA   Ever since you arrived you've had David on
            the brain.

ROBERT   It's this place. I'll be glad to leave. But the
            resemblance –

LINDA   Robert, everyone has a double. There's
            probably someone somewhere the image of
            me – although I find that hard to believe . . .
            do you think the man with his head on one
            side wanted to end it all . . . ?

ROBERT   He could be fed up with having his head on
                one side – the blind German on the other
                hand could have tripped. Actually, the man
                in the room below said he was hanging from
                their balcony.

LINDA   Good heavens! So close.

ROBERT   Closer than you think. The man below said
                he dropped from here.

LINDA   That's ridiculous. We'd have seen him.

ROBERT   We were in the bathroom. The door was
                unlocked. He could have come in. I noticed
                there was half a sandwich missing.

LINDA   Robert, are you suggesting that a total
                stranger came into our room, helped himself
                to a salmon sandwich and then decided
                to end it all and throw himself from our
                balcony?

ROBERT   No, that is ridiculous. My theory is that he
                jumped from higher up . . . misjudged it . . .
                landed on our balcony . . . had a sandwich
                . . . then decided to have another go . . .
                misjudged it again . . . landed on the balcony
                below . . . then decided to give the whole
                thing up.

LINDA   I'm not surprised. I think he must have
                decided by then that God intended him to
                live.

ROBERT   I hope so. (*Looks out.*) He'd make an awful
                mess.

LINDA   (*sighs*) Are you going to the Alhambra,
                Robert?

ROBERT   Yes, but before I go I think I'll have a word
              with that young man.,.

LINDA   (*alarmed*) What?

ROBERT   Give him a little fatherly advice.

              (*He passes back into the room.*)

LINDA   Oh, no – not your fatherly advice, Robert . . .

              (*She follows him in.* CLARE *has entered
              the sun terrace and has stretched out on a
              lounger.* JEREMY *enters. He moves around
              restlessly.*)

JEREMY   Do you know what I've just witnessed . . .
              coming by the front of the hotel?

CLARE   No?

JEREMY   (*lowers voice*) That nice woman – the one
              we met on our first night . . . in the arms of
              another man.

CLARE   What!

JEREMY   On one of the balconies. It was blatant – in
              full view – not an ounce of shame.

CLARE   It's a cry for help.

JEREMY   Is it?

CLARE;   She's been driven to it. It's a rebound.

JEREMY   Do you think so?

CLARE   You saw how much she loved him.

JEREMY	Who?
CLARE	Her husband. It's all that dreadful woman's fault. I may have to have a word.
JEREMY	I wouldn't. (*Pause.*) What time is it?
CLARE	Three-thirty. That's the third time you've asked me since we came up from the beach. What is it?
JEREMY	I feel tired . . .
CLARE	You've done nothing.
JEREMY	It must be the heat. Do you feel tired?
CLARE	No.
JEREMY	I feel like stretching out. (*Pause.*) Do you feel like stretching out?
CLARE	No.
JEREMY	I do.
CLARE	You can stretch out here.
JEREMY	I didn't mean here. I meant a siesta . . . They all do it.
CLARE	Do they?
JEREMY	They go to bed in the afternoon.
CLARE	(*stares*) Do you often go to bed in the afternoon?
JEREMY	Quite often.

CLARE	That must be quite a drawback for a serving officer. Suppose war's declared in the afternoon.
JEREMY	I wouldn't go to bed then – I'd be up all night. But then I'd be on active service. I'm not on active service at the moment . . . not yet . . . (*Winks.*)
CLARE	Don't start that.
JEREMY	Start what?
CLARE	That military jargon. It may be all right for the mess . . .
JEREMY	What jargon?
CLARE	Innuendos.
JEREMY	It wasn't an innuendo . . . well, not much of one . . .
CLARE	And what about this morning – after breakfast? When I'd barely digested my bacon and eggs. When you said, in a very heavy, suggestive tone, that you felt like, what was it 'a quick dash round the premises!'
JEREMY	I meant the hotel.
CLARE	No, you didn't. I was well aware what you meant. And now you've started again. What is it? Did the sight of those two on the balcony set you off?
JEREMY	Set me off?

CLARE   You're very prone to being set off since we
                got here. Almost at the push of a button.

JEREMY   Set me off! I'm on my honeymoon.

CLARE   You may be on your honeymoon – but there
                is a limit.

                (*She stands.*)

                And if you feel like 'a quick dash around the
                premises'. I suggest you go and inspect the
                hotel. I'm going for a walk.

                (*She exits. She brushes by* ROBERT *and* LINDA
                as they enter. ROBERT *and* LINDA *sit at an
                adjacent table.* ROBERT *observes* JEREMY'S
                dour expression.)

ROBERT   (*whispers*) It's not working out.

LINDA   (*sighs*) Don't interfere, Robert . . .

ROBERT   Too much sun. A word from the wise . . .

                (*He crosses to* JEREMY'S *table and leans
                over.*)

                Not working out?

JEREMY   (*stares*) What?

ROBERT   Let me give you some advice. You can
                have too much of a good thing. I know it's
                tempting but don't do it.

JEREMY   I beg your pardon.

ROBERT   You are not used to it. I suggest half an hour
                the first day . . . then an hour the next day . . .

then two hours and so on. After that, when
ever you feel like it and as much as you
want. But stop if you feel sore.

JEREMY   Really.

ROBERT   That's what I've always done. Now I'm
totally immune. I can go all day. And
I've been all over the world. I can take it
anywhere. In the tropics – up the Nile – on
the equator. You'll soon see me with my
shirt off . . .

(JEREMY *rises, looking thunderous.*)

Is something the matter?

JEREMY   You disgust me!

(JEREMY *storms off the terrace.* ROBERT
returns to LINDA.)

ROBERT   Well, that didn't go down very well.

LINDA   (*quietly*) I think he thought you were talking
about something else . . .

ROBERT   Something else?

LINDA   Not sun bathing . . . the other thing . . .

ROBERT   (*frowns*) The other thing. Ah, you mean
joint bank accounts . . . pre-nuptial
agreements . . .

LINDA   No – the other thing.

(ROBERT *stares. Realisation dawns.*)

ROBERT	Oh, that other thing. Pity we're not at home. I could have helped him. I've got a book on it.
LINDA	(*stares*) You have a book on it?
ROBERT	Yes.
LINDA	(*stares*) Have you read it?
ROBERT	Not all of it – it was pretty heavy going.
LINDA	I imagine it would be. Well, you'd better get off to the Alhambra. I'll sun bathe . . .
ROBERT	Right.

(ROBERT *exits*. LINDA *crosses towards the sunbeds. as she passes the ornamental shrub she hears a voice*.)

DAVID	(*out of sight*) Linda.

(LINDA *stops*.)

Don't turn round. I'm behind the bush.

LINDA	David! Robert's gone to the Alhambra but we must tread carefully – there's an elephant in the room.
DAVID	No – she's in reception.
LINDA	It's an expression, David. I was referring to something unresolved – an outstanding issue.
DAVID	Well, the outstanding issue is in reception organising an upgrade – then she'll want to inspect the room. That gives us our chance.

LINDA   (*gasps*) Brief encounter, David.

DAVID   It has to be.

LINDA   My heart's racing.

DAVID   So is mine.

               (LINDA *sees* AMY *enter the terrace. She
               moves off silently and crosses to the furthest
               sunbed and sits.*)

DAVID   (*unaware*) Now listen carefully . . .

               (CARLOS *who is passing stops and stares
               curiously into the bush.* AMY, *attracted by*
               CARLOS' *interest, joins him.*)

DAVID   I have to stay out of sight. She follows me
               everywhere. She's a shadow. She's a limpet.
               Ever tried to get rid of a limpet? It's almost
               impossible. After all these years . . . she's
               still obsessed with me. I don't know why . . .

               (DAVID'S *voice dies away as* AMY *appears
               around the bush.*)

AMY   What are you doing, David?

DAVID   What am I doing?

AMY   You appear to be talking to a bush.

DAVID   I was talking to you, Amy.

AMY   And who were you talking about, David?

               (DAVID *plays for time.*)

DAVID   (*low voice*) Who was I talking about?

*(He leads her to the front of the terrace,
well away from where* LINDA *is sunning
herself.)*

Who am I talking about! I'm talking about
her . . .

AMY   Her, the woman of whom I speak – whose
            name evades you?

            (She glances over DAVID'S *shoulder.)*

DAVID   Linda.

AMY   You do remember.

DAVID   It came back to me – when she gave me this
            searing glance . . .

AMY   Searing . . . You're lucky you still have your
            eyebrows, David.

DAVID   You can laugh but she hasn't got over me,
            Amy.

AMY   That can be difficult.

DAVID   She still has the hots for me after all these
            years . . .

AMY   Hence the searing. What are we going to do
            about it, David?

DAVID   Ignore her. Keep out of her way. That's all
            we can do . . .

            (They glance back at LINDA. *Her bare
            shoulders have appeared above the back of
            the lounger.)*

AMY	My God! She's gone topless!
DAVID	What!
AMY	She's got her buns out.
DAVID	(*sighs*) Do you have to be so crude, Amy?
AMY	Crude? I'm not the one who's taken her buns out.
DAVID	They're allowed to do it there. It's a topless area.
AMY	Then I'll take mine out . . .
	(*She starts to move off.*)
DAVID	No!
AMY	I just want to show her that you've nothing to leave home for.
DAVID	That's not necessary.
AMY	Or aren't my buns good enough?
DAVID	Your buns are lovely, Amy but there's no reason to put them in the shop window. Now sit down.
AMY	I think she's trying to entice you, David.
DAVID	I think you're right, Amy.
AMY	But it won't work.
DAVID	It certainly won't.

AMY	I mean, a man who has steak at home isn't going to go out for a beef burger.
DAVID	Too true.
	(*He sees* LINDA *exit.*)
	You can relax now – she's gone.
AMY	(*pause*) You didn't encourage her, did you, David?
DAVID	Certainly not. I can't think why she's even interested. Look at me. A man on a stick . . . with a creeping thing. I'm a wreck. When we get home leave me by the bins. I'm good for nothing else.
AMY	(*pause*) Would that be the black bin or the grey bin?
DAVID	Does it matter?
AMY	Well, the grey bin is for recycling . . . the black bin is landfill. Looking at you I'd say it's landfill.
DAVID	Why do you always do that?
AMY	Do what?
DAVID	Belittle me. That woman may be deluded but she senses something in me – a certain animal magnetism.
AMY	Animal what?
DAVID	Magnetism.

AMY

Chase me. All I can say is you'd better sit on that animal magnetism because if her husband finds out he might try to remove it with something sharp. Now, are you coming with me to reception? I have to pick up the key for the upgrade. They want us to inspect it.

DAVID

(*grumpily*) I have to see the hotel nurse. I'll catch up with you.

(AMY *stands up with him.*)

AMY

David, she's not the only one who thinks you're wonderful. I think you're wonderful. My fear is that if you find out how wonderful you really are . . . you may want to share it with the world . . .

(*She kisses him lightly on the cheek.* DAVID *exits, not sure whether to be pleased or annoyed by the last remark.* CLARE *and* JEREMY *have re-entered the terrace and have witnessed* AMY'S *farewell kiss.* JEREMY *sits at a nearby table but* CLARE *crosses to* AMY *as she prepares to leave.*)

CLARE

Do you mind if I have a word?

AMY

(*smiles*) Of course. I think I know what it's about. Why don't you sit down?

(*They both sit.*)

AMY

You're not happy, are you? Let me give you a little advice. (*Leans forward.*) Don't lose your sense of humour. You'll need it. They haven't got much – unless you find musical underpants funny. And try and keep your independence. That's what I've always done.

CLARE   Yes. I have noticed that but . . .

AMY   Don't give up driving – no matter what
             the cost. Have you ever tried parking with
             him sitting next to you? First it's the heavy
             breathing, then the grinding of teeth, then
             it's 'You're too far out, get in!'. Then it's,
             'Watch the kerb, watch those tyres!'. And
             when we've finished he's measuring the
             space from the kerb with his foot and I've
             got chest pains. But it's worth it. And
             another thing – tasting the wine.

CLARE   Tasting the wine?

AMY   Don't let him get away with it. He tried that
             with me. I was never allowed to choose the
             wine. I was never allowed to taste it. That
             was man's business. I'd watch him swirl it
             round his mouth and wait for the lofty nod
             of approval to the waiter, knowing all the
             time that he'd be perfectly happy with paint
             stripper.

CLARE   This is all very interesting but I didn't come
             for advice.

AMY   (*glances at* JEREMY) You didn't.

CLARE   I came to plead with you – to leave him
             alone.

AMY   What?

CLARE   You're destroying a marriage.

             (AMY *stares in surprise.*)

             A blissfully happy marriage with a radiant
             future. But that was yesterday. Then you

came alone with your free and easy ways –
you probably don't even realise what you've
done.

AMY   No, I don't.

CLARE   The truth is, you seem to have bewitched
           him.

           (AMY *glances over* CLARE'S *shoulder at the
           glum faced* JEREMY.)

AMY   I have? I didn't set out to.

CLARE   No – you appear to be quite careless with
           your favours. I've heard of women like you
           who come on holiday with the one intention
           of having a good time.

AMY   Well, I wouldn't say that exactly . . .

CLARE   The question is what are you going to do
           about it because that man is obsessed with
           you.

AMY   Is he?

           (*A second glance at* JEREMY.)

           I didn't encourage him.

CLARE   Of course you did. You flirted outrageously.

AMY   Did I? Well, it wasn't intentional . . . Do you
           think he has a preference for older women?

CLARE   Older women?

AMY   Yes.

CLARE	Well, I don't think the gap is so great.
AMY	You don't?
CLARE	No – and you have a lovely smile.
AMY	(*beams*) Do I?
CLARE	But please – don't turn it in his direction in future.
AMY	I'll try not to.

(CLARE *crosses to* JEREMY.)

CLARE   Jeremy . . .

(*She exits followed by* JEREMY. AMY
*stands for a moment, glowing from the
compliments? She looks down at her 'buns'
rather proudly. She straightens her dress,
pulls in her stomach and sticks out her
chest. Sways after* CLARE *and* JEREMY *then
remembers* CLARE'S *warning, turns abruptly
and exits in the other direction. The terrace
is now deserted.*)

(LINDA *enters the balcony. She leans over
and waves. She makes a beckoning gesture
and then a thumbs-up.*)

(ROBERT *appears behind her framed in the
French window. He regards her in silence.
He can't see the extent of the gestures but he
appears watchful. He disappears from the
opening.*)

(LINDA *straightens, her back stiffens. She's
heard something but she's not sure what.
She enters the room full of curiosity.*)

(*A moment later* DAVID *enters the balcony. He does a dance shuffle with his stick then hurls it away. He removes his glasses.* LINDA *enters furtively.*)

DAVID   I haven't much time.

(*He embraces her.*)

LINDA   Less than you think . . .

DAVID   Where were you?

LINDA   Checking the bathroom.

DAVID   (*cautiously*) The bathroom?

LINDA   He wasn't there.

DAVID   (*relaxes*) Good.

LINDA   He's in the wardrobe.

DAVID   What! Are you sure?

(*He slips on his dark glasses and picks up his stick.*)

LINDA   Yes. I can hear him breathing. I think he suspects, David.

(DAVID *makes for the door.*)

Where are you going?

DAVID   I'm getting out. I'm not going over that balcony again.

LINDA   Wait. I'll see if the coast's clear.

(*She exits into room.* DAVID *retreats from the door.* ROBERT *enters from the room.* DAVID *takes a further pace back.* ROBERT *looks at him in surprise.*)

ROBERT   Good heavens! Where did you come from?

(DAVID *starts. He wafts his stick about knocking china off the table, striking vases, etc.*)

DAVID   (*gutteral*) Vot is dis? Who sprechons?

ROBERT   I'm sorry – you're in the wrong room. You were probably meant to go next door. Our fault, shouldn't have left it open.

DAVID   I haf into zer wrong room kommen?

ROBERT   Afraid so.

DAVID   Der zimmer ist yours?

ROBERT   Yes.

DAVID   Vot a dummkopt!

ROBERT   No, an easy mistake to make – in your condition . . .

DAVID   (*appears to panic*) Vere am ich? Vere am ich?

(*He thrashes around.* ROBERT *grabs the end of the stick. They waltz around the balcony.*)

ROBERT   Steady, old chap. You're on the balcony.

DAVID   Zer balcony!

(*He seizes hold of* ROBERT *in terror.*)

ROBERT   Keep calm. Just sit for a moment. Get your breath.

(*He helps* DAVID *into a chair.* DAVID *bows in the wrong direction.*)

DAVID   Danke.

ROBERT   No. I'm over here . . .

(*He turns* DAVID *towards him. Regards him.*)

Sprechen sie English?

DAVID   Ja . . . bitte sprechen schlow . . .

ROBERT   I will.

DAVID   (*brightly*) Here ve go. Here ve go.

ROBERT   Very good.

DAVID   Vell played, sir.

ROBERT   Excellent.

DAVID   Rotten veather, old boy.

ROBERT   Well done.

DAVID   Cheeky Bugger.

ROBERT   Yes . . . I can see you have an extensive vocabulary . . .

(*He takes* DAVID'S *hand and touches his chest.*)

	Robert. And you?
DAVID	Fritz.
ROBERT	And vere do you come from, Fritz?
DAVID	(*cautiously*) Deutschland.
ROBERT	Whereabouts in Deutschland?
DAVID	(*pause*) Ich bin ein Berliner.
ROBERT	Ah, Berlin. Hitler never cared for it. Mind you, he was a bit of a bastard. Although that was a brilliant thrust through the Ardennes.

(*He studies* DAVID.)

Hope you don't mind me staring – of course, you wouldn't know would you? But you do have an incredible likeness to someone I met here years ago. He was a bigger bastard than Hitler. He tried to run off with my wife.

(DAVID *looks appalled.*)

DAVID	Der housefrau?
ROBERT	Ja. I swore that if I ever met him again I'd kill him.
DAVID	Gut.
ROBERT	You agree with those sentiments.
DAVID	Ja.
ROBERT	Render him kaput?
DAVID	Ja – kaput.

ROBERT	You do remind me of him. You don't have any relations in England?
DAVID	Nein.
ROBERT	Then you must have a double.
DAVID	A doppel?
ROBERT	Yes . . . unless. Do you mind?

(He leans forward and removes DAVID's glasses.)

Yes, as I thought. It is you, isn't it, David?

DAVID	No.

(He backs away. ROBERT closes with him.)

DAVID	It's just someone who looks like me.
ROBERT	No . . . I'd never mistake you for anyone else. I have good cause to remember you, David. And do you remember my last words to you?
DAVID	You said you'd kill me if you found me near your wife . . . whose name evades me at the moment . . .
ROBERT	Linda. She's locked herself in the bathroom.
DAVID	I wouldn't call that close.
ROBERT	Close enough. She's locked herself in because she doesn't want to see what's going to happen.

(ROBERT's *hands begin to clench and unclench.*)

DAVID   What's going to happen? No – don't answer that. Robert, you keep making fists . . .

ROBERT   Yes, that's got worse over the years – I can't help it.

DAVID   Have you thought of anger management?

           (*They have begun to circle the balcony.*)

ROBERT   I'm not angry.

DAVID   You're not?

ROBERT   I'm quite calm.

DAVID   Well, that's a step in the right direction.

ROBERT   I feel that revenge is a dish best eaten cold.

DAVID   That's premeditation.

ROBERT   It certainly is . . .

DAVID   They'll get you for that.

ROBERT   It will be an accident. You'll just . . .

           (*He makes a diving motion with his hand.*)

DAVID   I'm not going to go . . .

           (*He repeats the diving motion.*)

           I'll shout – I'll struggle. They won't believe I fell by accident.

ROBERT   Not by accident. You're forgetting,
              David. There's a man at this hotel already
              considered a suicide risk – a man who looks
              rather like you. Everyone will think he's
              finally done it . . . (*Cold smile.*) Capeesh.

DAVID   That's not German.

ROBERT   No, but neither are you, David,
              unfortunately.

DAVID   Can't we talk about this?

ROBERT   By all means. Do you dream, David?

DAVID   Well, sometimes.

ROBERT   I do. Do you dream that you're in a public
              place – a board meeting, a conference and
              you suddenly become aware that you're
              without your trousers?

DAVID   No.

ROBERT   I do. And do you know when those dreams
              started? After I met you all those years ago.
              And here you are again!

DAVID   Robert, there's a perfectly simple, innocent
              explanation.

ROBERT   If you're innocent why were you pretending
              to be a German tourist – a blind German
              tourist.

DAVID   Partially sighted. Because when I saw you
              I remembered your last words to me. I was
              terrified and it was the first thing that came
              into my head.

ROBERT   No, you were terrified because you were
riddled with guilt. You knew Linda was here
– a woman alone – and you stalked her.

DAVID   I'm not a stalker – I wasn't even in
the scouts. Our meeting was a pure
coincidence. I knew someone who found his
grandmother's wedding ring –

ROBERT   It wasn't a coincidence. It was planned.
You knew I was in Rome . . . and you
sprang your trap. If I hadn't come back
unexpectedly . . .

DAVID   Robert, it was a chance meeting. Amy and I
came here for a short break. I had no idea –

ROBERT   Amy isn't here, David.

DAVID   She is.

ROBERT   No, because you wouldn't have planned
this with Amy in attendance. I remember
Amy. You wouldn't have risked having your
trousers hanging from the bougainvillea and
Linda certainly wouldn't have risked a pie in
the face.

DAVID   I swear she's here. If she isn't I'll eat those
flowers.

ROBERT   David, if she is here – I'll eat them.

DAVID   (*hopefully*) Will you?

ROBERT   But even if she was here it doesn't explain
one small item.

DAVID   What?

ROBERT	What were you doing on our balcony?
DAVID	What was I doing on your balcony? What was I doing on your balcony?
ROBERT	That's what I said.

(DAVID *is playing for time.*)

DAVID	I was on your balcony . . . because . . .

(AMY *pops her head around the French window.*)

AMY	There you are, David. You beat me to it. Well, what do you think to our upgrade?

(DAVID *wrenches himself free of* ROBERT.)

DAVID	Not too bad. I haven't seen the bathroom yet.
AMY	There's someone in there.

(*She sees* ROBERT *standing with his mouth open.*)

Oh, hello, Robert. Moving out? Come and look at the bed, David. It's massive . . .

(*She exits.* ROBERT *remains dumbfounded.*

DAVID *moves to the door. Turns back. He hands the bowl of flowers to* ROBERT.)

DAVID	Bon appetite . . .

(DAVID *exits. Curtain.*)

.

Scene Two

Hotel. Early evening.

The terrace is deserted.

DAVID *is alone on the balcony. He is leaning over the railings and peering down below.* AMY *enters through the French door and freezes.*

AMY	Come away from that rail . . . dear.
DAVID	(*turns*) Why did you call me that?
AMY	What?
DAVID	Dear. The last time you called me that was after I'd fallen down the cellar steps.
AMY	I can call you dear if I like . . .
	(*She leads him away from the rail and sits him at the table.*)
	We are married.
DAVID	Did they tell you how much we'll have to pay for this place?
AMY	Yes. (*Pause.*) I had to see the General Manager . . . .
DAVID	And?
AMY	You've been identified, David.
DAVID	(*uneasily*) What do you mean . . . identified?
AMY	As the man who ran away from his rescuers last night. They showed me a picture taken

by one of the guests. It's you all right. They said you were trying to kill yourself.

DAVID   I wasn't trying to kill myself!

AMY   Then what were you doing swinging from the balcony?

DAVID   (*hesitates*) I was thinking about it . . .

AMY   But you changed your mind.

DAVID   Yes.

AMY   That's what the manager thought.

DAVID   I suppose he wants me to leave.

AMY   No, he'd like you to see a psychiatrist.

DAVID   What!

AMY   They have one here who speaks perfect English.

DAVID   No!

AMY   David, he's concerned about you. He's afraid you may try again and alarm the guests. They have a name in Spanish for your condition . . .

DAVID   And what's that?

AMY   Loco.

DAVID   Loco! I'm not mad.

AMY   It runs in the family.

DAVID   No, it doesn't.

AMY   There was your Uncle Fred. Thought his
               head was on the wrong way round – nearly
               broke his neck trying to put it right.

DAVID   That was a passing delusion.

AMY   It was more than that, David. He wore his
               clothes back to front.

DAVID   Well, you haven't seen me doing that, have
               you?

AMY   No but the mad can be crafty. Dickens' mad
               man used to go into empty fields and laugh
               wildly to himself.

DAVID   Do I go into empty fields and laugh wildly
               to myself?

AMY   How would I know? And you said yourself
               you were having a breakdown, dear.

               (DAVID *frowns at the word 'dear'.*)

DAVID   I'm not having a nervous breakdown!

AMY   You're not the same person. I realised last
               night when you came to bed that you'd
               reached the end of your powers.

DAVID   What!

AMY   But that doesn't mean you have to kill
               yourself.

DAVID   Amy, I'm not going to kill myself because of
               that!

AMY	(*quietly*) You were trying again this afternoon.
DAVID	No.
AMY	When I came onto the balcony this afternoon I sensed there'd been a struggle – I didn't realise that Robert was trying to restrain you.
DAVID	Restrain me? Did he say that?
AMY	No. But it was obvious. I know you, David. You saw this sumptuous apartment – one you could never afford – and you'd be consumed with a sense of failure – what with that and coming to the end of your powers. You must have felt, what's left?
DAVID	Well, there's always bingo. What did Robert say exactly?
AMY	He's changed. He seemed very concerned about you – about the state of your health. He asked a lot of questions.
DAVID	(*warily*) What sort of questions?
AMY	Whether you could still get about. How fit you were. How far the creeping thing had crept. (*Pause.*) I couldn't help noticing how his hands open and close whilst he's talking. Perhaps he's having trouble with the Euro.
DAVID	Well, we shan't be seeing them again now they've gone to the Alhambra.
AMY	We shall, we're having drinks with them this evening.

DAVID   What!

AMY   It was Robert's idea. Apparently he can't
            see enough of you. It's David this and David
            that.

DAVID   I'm not up to it, Amy. I thought a quiet
            evening with room service . . .

AMY   He'll be disappointed. He suggested a
            farewell drink.

DAVID   (*hesitates*) It was farewell . . . ?

AMY   Yes.

DAVID   (*suspiciously*) What did he mean . . .
            farewell?

AMY   What does it usually mean?

DAVID   (*sighs*) I don't know about this, Amy. I can
            hardly walk at the moment,.

AMY   Well, we can't afford room service – not
            after we've paid for the upgrade.

DAVID   I'm not really up to it, Amy.

AMY   I had thought about that and I have a
            surprise for you . . .

            (*She opens both the French doors. She
            exits.* DAVID *watches her curiously. There's
            the pip-pip of a motor horn off. A moment
            later* AMY *passes through the doors on a
            wheelchair.*

            DAVID *stares in horror.*)

DAVID	Where did that come from?
AMY	It belongs to the hotel. They've let me borrow it.
DAVID	I'm not going in that! I'm not decrepit. What will people think?
AMY	I know what Robert will think. He'll realise the gravity of the situation . . .
DAVID;	(*hesitates*) That's true I suppose . . . Well, perhaps just for this evening . . . until I get the strength back in my legs . . .

(AMY *helps him into the chair.*)

AMY	(*temptingly*) It's got a little horn.

(DAVID *pips the horn. He propels himself forward.*)

Careful, David – we don't want you to go through the railings . . .

(DAVID *begins to reverse.*)

AMY	(*admiringly*) David, you were born to drive one of these.

(DAVID *gives her a doubtful glance and exits followed by* AMY. *Sound of pip-pip off.* CLARE *is sitting by a table far stage left with a drink in her hand. She doesn't look happy.* JEREMY *enters.*)

JEREMY	I've just seen the man we met last night. He was with the other woman again.
CLARE	No! And she virtually promised . . .

JEREMY   He was in a wheelchair.

CLARE   What!

JEREMY   He was in a wheelchair.

CLARE   My God! What is she doing to him?

JEREMY   I don't know. (*Enviously.*) Must be having a
              good time.

CLARE   I beg your pardon?

JEREMY   (*guiltily*) I mean, he'll think he's having a
              good time but he'll be wrong.

CLARE   He certainly is. It's probably guilt.

JEREMY   Guilt?

CLARE   Eating into him. The wages of sin, Jeremy.
              It's this place. They're all at it. I saw his
              wife holding hands with the man with the
              moustache. Completely shameless. It must
              be the effect of Sangria and the sea air. It
              has some sort of coarsening effect.

JEREMY   (*gloomily*) It hasn't affected me . . .

CLARE   Hasn't it? What did you say to me before
              we came down to dinner? Whilst I was
              changing?

JEREMY   I don't remember.

CLARE   I do. You said 'I feel like a quick burst
              on my banjo'. Is that how they talk in the
              officers' mess?

JEREMY   No.

CLARE   No – it's this place. It used to be poetry now
                 it's 'I feel like a quick burst on my banjo'.

JEREMY   (*pause*) Do you think they're wife-
                 swoppers?

CLARE   Why? Are you thinking of joining in?

JEREMY   No! Certainly not.

CLARE   I feel for the wife. She's being drawn into it.
                 You can see she's reluctant. The man with
                 the moustache obviously has money – that's
                 a powerful aphrodisiac. Whilst I believe her
                 husband has financial problems. There's a
                 rumour that he tried to commit suicide.

                 (ROBERT *and* LINDA *enter hand-in-hand.*
                 They sit at a far table stage right.)

JEREMY   (*whispers*) They're holding hands.

CLARE   He's probably afraid she'll get away.

                 (ROBERT *stands.*)

ROBERT   I'll see what happened to that waiter . . .

                 (ROBERT *exits.* CLARE *hurries across to*
                 LINDA. JEREMY *sighs and rolls his eyes.*)

CLARE   (*low voice*) Don't give in now.

LINDA   (*nervously*) I shan't.

                 (CLARE *glances after* ROBERT.)

CLARE   He's obviously not your type.

LINDA   That thought has occurred to me . . .

CLARE	Remember it was for better or worse, It may seem a little worse at the moment but it will pass. I know he doesn't look much and he has tried to kill himself but that's because of his money problems . . .
LINDA	I didn't know he had money problems. He told me he had a numbered account in Switzerland.
CLARE	Then why does he have problems?
LINDA	Perhaps he's forgotten the number.
CLARE	There must be a reason. You must have noticed his frayed cuffs.
LINDA	Are they frayed?
CLARE	Surely you've seen them whilst you were ironing.
LINDA	(*appalled*) Ironing?
CLARE	Of course a wife isn't always aware of these things. You can be too close to someone. But you must be aware of that terrible woman.
LINDA	Terrible? Yes . . . that does describe her.
CLARE	What does he see in her?
LINDA	I've often wondered. But she was a good mother.
CLARE	(*stares*) A good mother? Why should that attract him?
LINDA	Er . . . I have no idea.

(ROBERT *enters with* CARLOS *who is carrying a tray bearing champagne and glasses.* CLARE *returns to her table but continues to eye them narrowly.* ROBERT *looks at his watch.*)

ROBERT   They're late. Probably having a last look at the sea. I'll see if I can find them.

LINDA   (*hurriedly*) I'll come with you.

(*They cross to the steps.* ROBERT *takes her hand.* LINDA *catches* CLARE'S *eye and looks guilty. They exit.*)

CLARE   Did you see that? The way he hangs on to her.

(DAVID *enters in the wheelchair pushed by* AMY. AMY *studiously avoids looking at* JEREMY.)

CLARE   (*low voice*) My God! What has she done to him?

(AMY *directs* DAVID *as far away from the young couple as possible.*)

DAVID   Champagne. Looks as if Robert's beaten us.

(CLARE *stands.*)

JEREMY   Where are you going?

CLARE   To get my mobile. Stay here.

(CLARE *exits.* AMY *looks around.*)

AMY   David, there are some cakes on that table . . .

DAVID   Must have been left over from tea . . .

AMY   (*pause*) I don't suppose they'll miss them . . .

DAVID   You can't be serious.

AMY   I haven't eaten all day.

DAVID   Why not?

AMY   We can't afford it – not and pay the
               supplement.

DAVID   Well, wait until dinner.

AMY   Dinner. That won't fill me. There's more
               plate than food and we can't afford the
               extras.

DAVID   That's because it's gourmet, Amy. Not that
               you'd appreciate that.

AMY   That's a strange remark from a man whose
               favourite dish is toad-in-the-hole . . .

               (*She looks longingly at the cakes. Becomes
               awestruck.*)

AMY   David, do you know what that is – the big
               cake?

DAVID   (*sighs*) I've no idea.

AMY   I don't know what they call it in Spanish but
               that's an elephant's foot.

DAVID   A what?

AMY	An elephant's foot. Choux pastry crammed with fresh cream – and so big you can barely get your jaws round it.
DAVID	Well, that shouldn't worry you but you're not having it.
AMY	David . . . My mouth's watering . . .
DAVID	Let it water. You can't afford any more weight.
AMY	(*pause*) I don't look so bad.
DAVID	It's a long time since anyone said that about you.
AMY	On the contrary . . . would it surprise you to know that I'm having to discourage someone at this very moment . . .
DAVID	(*half laughs*) What? You? Not Robert?
AMY	No – certainly not. I don't think his hands are opening and closing because of me.
DAVID	Well, who?
AMY	(*lowers voice*) He's looking at us . . .
	(DAVID *stares across at* JEREMY.)
DAVID	Not him.
AMY	Yes.
DAVID	He's just got married!
AMY	I know. I think he regrets it.

DAVID   But she's very attractive.

AMY   I know. He must be looking for something
                 different.

DAVID   My God! He'll certainly get it.

AMY   What do you mean by that?

DAVID   You're old enough to be his mother.

DAVID   I know that. But some men are attracted to
                 older women.

DAVID   Yes, but they're fashionable, good looking
                 women.

AMY   What am I? Something the cat brought in?

DAVID   No – but you're talking about film stars –
                 those sort of people.

AMY   No, I'm not.

DAVID   How do you know he's attracted to you?

AMY   His wife told me. She's obviously worried.

DAVID   I'm not surprised. She should get him to the
                 opticians.

AMY   David, could you suppress your
                 astonishment, just for a moment? Don't
                 worry, I'm not looking for a toy boy. I intend
                 to discourage him. I'll do it now whilst his
                 wife isn't there. I know what it feels like to
                 be humiliated . . .

                 (AMY *rises and crosses to* JEREMY's *table*.)

AMY   (*smiles*) Hello . . .

JEREMY   (*uneasily*) Hello.

AMY   (*leans forward*) It's not to be, is it?

JEREMY   What?

AMY   You and me. It's out of the question, isn't it?

JEREMY   (*stares*) Were you thinking about it?

AMY   Weren't you? Please – don't think the idea
               isn't attractive but I do have a husband and
               I'm old enough to be your mother.

               (JEREMY *looks across at* DAVID, *who's
               watching them closely.*)

JEREMY   What's the matter with him?

AMY   Worn out.

JEREMY   And now it's me.

AMY   Pardon?

JEREMY   You're old enough to be my mother.

AMY   I've just said that.

JEREMY   Doesn't that worry you?

AMY   Yes but it doesn't appear to worry you.
               That's why I thought I'd have a word.

JEREMY   My God! You're voracious.

AMY   I'm not voracious. If I was voracious I'd
               have eaten that cake. All I'm asking you to

do is exercise a little self control. You've
married a beautiful girl.

JEREMY   I know.

AMY   And I'm old enough to be her mother too.
                You'll get over me . . . in time. It'll pass.
                It'll fade with the sun tan. It's this place –
                the smell of the bougainvillaea – the throb
                of guitars on the beach – the driftwood
                fires – the gentle surge of the sea . . . You'll
                forget me . . .

                (*She pats him lightly on the cheek.* JEREMY
                *watches her open mouthed as she returns to
                her table.*)

DAVID   Well, did you discourage him?

AMY   I did my best only he appears to be besotted
                with me. Either that or he's half-witted.

DAVID   My money's on half-witted.

AMY   I'm not sure. It could be an Aubrey
                Broadbent situation. They say he was never
                the same after I married you.

DAVID   He looked the same to me.

AMY   Mother always wanted me to marry him.
                I'll tell you something I've never told you
                before. My mother wept when I told her you
                and I were engaged.

DAVID   I'll tell you something I've never told you
                before. So did mine.

AMY   The devious old bat. She said I was like a
           daughter to her! How two-faced. It must run
           in the family . . .

           (ROBERT *and* LINDA *return.*)

ROBERT   Ah, there you are. Have some champagne,
           you two.

DAVID   Thank you, Robert.

AMY   You look nice and brown, Linda.

LINDA   Do I?

AMY   I saw you sunbathing. And I saw that you'd
           got your buns –

           (DAVID *gives her a warning glance.*)

           – that you were getting an all over tan.

LINDA   I think it looks so much nicer.

AMY   Yes . . . or it's two poached eggs on toast . . .

LINDA   Do you go topless?

AMY   No. David feels it's a view only he should
           feast his eyes on.

           (DAVID *almost chokes on his champagne.*)

           He can be insanely jealous . . . .

ROBERT   Sorry to see you in a wheelchair, David.

DAVID   A cross I have to bear, Robert.

ROBERT	Having a job getting about . . . climbing stairs . . . that sort of thing.?
DAVID	Stairs are out of the question I'm afraid.
	(ROBERT'S *manner has become faintly questioning.*)
AMY	(*brightly*) We're getting a stair lift.
ROBERT	No sliding down drainpipes then?
	(*Everyone laughs somewhat uneasily.*)
DAVID	Certainly not.
ROBERT	I suppose you need Amy with you most of the time . . . ?
DAVID	Oh, yes . . . we're almost inseparable . . .
AMY	I am thinking of putting in for a carer's allowance.
	(DAVID *frowns.*)
ROBERT	Then you're not able to travel alone . . . ?
LINDA	My, isn't it warm up here?
DAVID	No, those days are over, I'm afraid.
AMY	Well, you did manage –
	(LINDA *continues trying to interrupt.*)
LINDA	Don't you feel warm, Amy?
AMY	No but I must say you do look a little flushed.

ROBERT Well, those days certainly aren't over for Linda. Only this week she –

LINDA I think it would be cooler by the sea. Why don't we go on the beach?

ROBERT Linda, you're forgetting David's wheelchair.

LINDA Oh, yes. Sorry, David.

DAVID That's all right, Linda. (*Bravely.*) One gets used to an infirmity . . .

(*He gives* LINDA *a sly wink.* ROBERT *looks across at* JEREMY. *He lowers his voice.*)

ROBERT Should we ask that young chap over to share our champagne?

(*Everyone looks nervous.*)

I think he'd had a touch of the sun. It's made him a little strange. I feel sorry for the poor devil.

DAVID I wouldn't, Robert.

ROBERT Why not?

DAVID He has this thing for Amy.

LINDA For Amy? Priceless!

(*A peal of laughter from* LINDA. *All join in but* AMY, *who is not amused.*)

ROBERT A thing! Well, it's a long time since you've had a thing, hey, David?

DAVID So long I've almost forgotten, Robert.

ROBERT   And you used to be such a ladies' man . . .

DAVID   Did I? That was before this . . . But it has
              its consolations. I enjoy listening to music
              these days . . .

ROBERT   You've aged, David.

LINDA   (*brightly*) Should we go to the bar?

AMY   I'll say he's aged. I look at him sometimes
              and I think 'My God, you've aged – you've
              more lines than Clapham Junction'.

DAVID   (*frowns*) Well, I wouldn't say that.

AMY   I've removed all the mirrors. He kept
              looking into them and seeing his father.

ROBERT   So, it's listening to music, is it, David?

DAVID   (*nods*) Classic FM. Schubert, Beethoven,
              Brahms.

ROBERT   No more a-roving.

DAVID   No.

ROBERT   And you so enjoyed the company of a pretty
              woman . . .

DAVID   A thing of the past, Robert.

ROBERT   (*glances at* LINDA) So, you no longer admire
              the female form?

LINDA   I think I'll get my shawl.

AMY   I thought you were warm?

LINDA	I've gone cold.
DAVID	What were you saying, Robert?
ROBERT	I asked if you still admired the female form.
DAVID	(*shakes head*) Not in my condition. To be honest, I prefer a good sunset these days . . .
LINDA	(*quickly*) There's a good sunset from the other terrace . . . Should we . . . ?
AMY	No, we can't keep moving David around. He gets dizzy.

(DAVID *scowls.*)

And what about me? It's no joke pushing him around. It's wearing me out. It was a struggle getting him out of the bath tonight.

DAVID	(*indignantly*) It wasn't a struggle.
ROBERT	He has trouble getting out of the bath?
AMY	I'll say. If things get much worse we'll need a block and tackle.
DAVID	That won't be necessary.
AMY	Well, it's either that or filling the bath to the top and floating him over the edge.
ROBERT	I didn't think things were as bad as that.
AMY	He hides it. He's very brave.
LINDA	Oh, there's that strange woman . . .

(CLARE *has entered stage left.*)

Should we go. She will stare at me . . .

CLARE   Jeremy.

(JEREMY *rises and follows* CLARE *who crosses to confront* ROBERT.)

ROBERT   (*midly surprised*) Yes?

CLARE   Perhaps you'd like to see this picture.

(*She hands her mobile to* ROBERT.)

You'll see how radiant they look. How full of joy and expectation. Now look at them . . .

(ROBERT *and* AMY *look at the picture, then at* LINDA *and* DAVID, *and then back again.*)

That's what you two have done. I hope you're proud of yourselves.

(ROBERT *rises to his feet.*)

ROBERT   When was this taken?

CLARE   Only last night!

(CLARE *snatches the phone from him . . . and storms out.*)

ROBERT   Last night!

JEREMY   (*sneers*) Don't look so surprised, after all, you're the ringleader.

(JEREMY *follows* CLARE. ROBERT *sits, stunned for a moment.*)

ROBERT   Ringleader.

LINDA	I think I'll go and freshen up . . .
	(*She edges towards the exit, stage right.*)
AMY	(*rises*) I think I'll join you . . .
	(LINDA *exits.* AMY *selects the 'elephant's foot' from the other table.*)
DAVID	(*anxiously*) Don't leave me, Amy.
AMY	This won't take long, David.
	(AMY *exits after* LINDA. DAVID *watches her go then turns his head to find* ROBERT *towering over him.*)
DAVID	Now, Robert, you're making fists again.
ROBERT	I know.
DAVID	You wouldn't hit a man in a wheelchair . . .
ROBERT	I don't intend to . . .
	(*He begins to push the wheelchair across the terrace.*)
DAVID	Where are we going?
ROBERT	I'm not going anywhere.
DAVID	Where am I going?
ROBERT	To have a last look at the sea. You did say you preferred a good sunset . . .
DAVID	You'll have a job getting me down those steps.

(They have paused at the exit to the steps.)

ROBERT   I won't because I'm not going.

DAVID;   What!

ROBERT   Goodbye, David . . .

              (He shoves the wheelchair. DAVID *and the wheelchair disappear off. Wild shouts from* DAVID. *Frantic pipping from the horn. Sounds of crash.* AMY *enters from stage right. She's wiping her hands.)*

AMY   *(concerned)* Where's David?

ROBERT   *(turns)* Gone for a ride. Don't worry – he's survived – although I can't say the same for the wheelchair . . .

ROBERT   *(He holds out his hand.)*

              Well, goodbye, Amy. We're off to the Alhambra. We shan't meet again.

AMY   No . . . Excuse my creamy fingers.

ROBERT   Certainly. Bye Amy.

              *(*AMY *watches* ROBERT *exit.)*

AMY   Bye, Robert . . .

              (She crosses to the table and helps herself to another cake. She begins to eat it. DAVID *emerges from the stairwell. His clothes are crumpled and ripped. He staggers across to* AMY, *leaning on tables and chairs, trying to win sympathy.)*

DAVID   He pushed me down the steps.

AMY   Yes.

DAVID   I could have been killed. There could have been a tragedy.

AMY   What makes you think it would have been a tragedy?

DAVID   If that waiter with the bad feet hadn't been in the way – he broke my fall . . .

             (*His voice dies away as the* WAITER *drags himself onto the terrace. He pulls himself upright. Straightens his uniform. Glares across at* DAVID.)

WAITER   (*snarls*) Inglese!

             (*He makes a savage gesture and exits.*)

DAVID   What was that all about?

AMY   He's thrown you the five, David.

DAVID   What does that mean?

AMY   Endless bad luck.

DAVID   I think it's just started.

AMY   Just look at you. Do you know who you remind me of? Old Towser.

DAVID   (*stares*) Your mother's old dog?

AMY   Yes. When he was twelve and so full of arthritis we had to lift him in and out of the car he made his way through three back

gardens to where Buttons was in season.
He chewed his way through a stout wooden
fence and seduced Buttons – had a bucket of
water thrown over him and returned home to
die with a canine smile on his face. (*Sighs.*)
Just look at you. What am I going to do with
you, David?

DAVID   I don't know, Amy?

AMY   You've ruined those clothes. Straighten up.

               (*She begins to straighten his clothes. They
               are quite close. All at once there's the sound
               of 'Jingle Bells'! It grows louder.*)

AMY   My God! You're wearing them!

DAVID   I thought it might raise a smile if nothing
               else . . .

AMY   (*shakes head*) David . . .

DAVID   I think the feeling's returning, Amy.

AMY   Really?

DAVID   (*putting a hand on hers*) I think I'm getting
               my appetite back.

AMY   Are you? Then have a cake.

               (*She weighs the cake thoughtfully in her
               hand for a moment and then hands it to him.
               He begins to chew it mournfully. They are
               both eating as the lights fade.*)

PROPERTY LIST

ACT ONE

Scene One

Set: Tables and chairs on the stage level terrace. Unspecified number. An additional table and chairs on the balcony USR. Three sun loungers.

Glasses and menus on terrace table.

Personal: Jacket (DAVID)

Camera with flash (JEREMY)

Hotel room key (LINDA)

Tray (CARLOS)

Mobile phone (DAVID)

Mobile phone (AMY)

Tray with smoked salmon sandwiches and Champagne (CARLOS)

Pad and pen (CARLOS)

Towel (LINDA)

Scene Two

Set: Bowl of flowers on table

Personal: Sun hat (LINDA)

Dark Glasses (LINDA)

Hand mirror (LINDA)

Robe (DAVID)

Walking stick (DAVID)

Dark glasses (DAVID)

Tray with coffee and cakes for two (CARLOS)

ACT TWO

Scene One

Set: Bowl of flowers on terrace table

China/vases on balcony table

Personal: Wrist watch (CLARE)

Scene Two

Personal: Drink (CLARE)

Tray with Champagne and glasses (CARLOS)

Wheelchair with horn attached (DAVID)

Wrist watch (ROBERT)

Tray with cream cakes (AMY)

Mobile phone (CLARE)

Handkerchief (AMY)